Everybody's GRAMMAR

Book 1

James Sale

Keith Selby

Mary Green

Bruce Martin

Liz Martin

Acknowledgements

James Sale and Keith Selby hereby assert their moral rights to be identified as the authors of this work in accordance with the Copyright, Designs and Patents Act 1988.

Editor: Andrew Brown   Layout artist: Patricia Hollingsworth
Cover image: Digital Vision Ltd.   Cover design: Kim Ashby, Ed Gallagher
Illustrations: Tony O'Donnell – Graham Cameron Illustration, Gary Clifford – The Drawing Room

© 1998 Folens Limited, on behalf of the authors.

Every effort has been made to contact copyright holders of material used in this book. If any have been overlooked, we will be pleased to make any necessary arrangements.

British Library Cataloguing in Publication Data. A catalogue record for this book is available from the British Library.

First published 1998 by Folens Limited, Dunstable and Dublin.
Folens Limited, Albert House, Apex Business Centre, Boscombe Road, Dunstable, LU5 4RL, England.

ISBN 1 86202485–5

Printed in Singapore by Craft Print.

Texts and sources

This is a book about various aspects of grammar, but it draws upon a wide range of sources – from poems and plays, through to novels and newspaper articles. As a result the publishers wish to thank the following:

Page 6   *A Sunrise on the Veldt*, from *This Was the Old Chief's Country* by Doris Lessing (Curtis Brown).

Page 9   *Ballad of the Bikkly Boy* by James Sale.

Page 17   *Under Milk Wood* by Dylan Thomas (JM Dent & David Higham Associates).

Page 63   *Teacher Said* by Judith Nicholls (Faber & Faber).

Page 72   *Abandoning* by Samih al-Qasim from *Victims of a Map* translated by Abdullah al-Udhair (Al Saqi Books).

Page 77   *Danny* by JM Synge, reprinted in *Plays, Poems and Prose of J Millington Synge* (Everyman, Dent).

Page 80   *Hush-a-bye* by Susan Moody (Macmillan & Co).

Page 85   'Charcot-Marie Tooth disease' story based upon an extract from the *Poole Advertiser*, Vol III issue 281, September 18, 1997.

Page 88   *First Day at School* by Barry Heath from *Poetry Show 1* (Macmillan/ Nelson).

Page 90   *Writing* by Jan Dean from *Poetry Street 3* (Longman).

Page 91   *Mummy Tells Joseph about the Princess* by James Sale.

Introduction

Folens' *Everybody's Grammar* is a comprehensive course for pupils between the ages of 11–14, and aims to make language skills and usage as accessible and lively as possible. 'Grammar' here is taken to include a wide range of definitions and ideas; at its most basic, it is the heart of language – the letter – which can denote both sound and symbol (and this is where all three books start). At its most expansive, it denotes the whole system of language – the holistic text – of which letter, sound, phrase, sentence and so on are constituent parts. For this reason, there are poems, prose and script extracts, studies of genre and extended writing activities to run alongside the individual elements that make up the whole.

In addition, the books provide practical and helpful sections designed to aid the teacher in developing the pupil's skills and understanding.
There are:

- *regular reviews of skills covered previously*
- *tests and exercises*
- *longer assignments requiring pupils to practise what they have learned*
- *helpful menus of targets so that pupils can set realistic goals.*

Each book begins with a section called 'Starting points' which enables pupils to review where they are with regard to language knowledge and usage. In Book One, for example, the questions 'What is grammar?' and 'What is language?' are addressed. In the later books, pupils are tested on what they might reasonably be expected to know at that stage in their education.

The books broadly follow a framework of:

- *word level work*
- *sentence level work*
- *whole text level work.*

It is not the intention of the authors that this should be a straitjacket, it is merely a useful way of providing a sense of how language consists of a series of interlocking parts.Work on paragraphs, for example, appears in 'Shaping texts' but, equally, it could appear in 'Shaping sentences'.

In essence, the books are based on the notion that this is a 'grammar' that teachers will recognise, made up of those labels children ought to know to enable them to use language more effectively and imaginatively.

Contents

What is language?

Language is ... words.

Make a list of as many words as you can find that are about language in the word-search below.

A	S	B	U	S	M	L	V	J	N	T	E	U	E	C	B	A	Q
D	U	U	R	P	V	V	G	K	O	N	L	T	N	T	S	N	E
J	R	M	N	E	O	H	U	R	U	A	B	B	T	E	E	T	S
E	U	Y	U	L	V	Q	U	A	N	N	A	R	V	B	N	O	A
C	A	N	O	L	A	D	T	M	W	O	L	E	O	A	T	N	R
T	S	O	N	I	M	O	A	M	O	S	L	V	W	H	E	Y	H
I	E	N	O	N	M	Q	N	A	R	N	Y	E	E	P	N	M	P
V	H	Y	R	G	O	U	Q	R	D	O	S	M	L	L	C	G	W
E	T	S	P	R	C	J	M	G	B	C	R	Z	I	A	E	Z	G

Tasks

 Choose any word and explain to a friend what it means.

 Language consists of:

Information: She parked the car.

Ideas: She had considered taking the bus.

Feelings: She was angry because she was late.

Read the following passage and, in pairs, list examples of information, ideas and feelings.

It came into his mind that he should shoot it and end its pain; and he raised the gun. Then he lowered it again. The buck could no longer feel; its fighting was a mechanical protest of the nerves. But it was not that which made him put down the gun. It was a swelling feeling of rage and misery and protest that expressed itself in the thought: if I had not come it would have died like this: so why should I interfere? All over the bush things like this happen; they happen all the time; this is how life goes on, by living things dying in anguish. He gripped the gun between his knees and felt in his own limbs the myriad swarming pain of the twitching animal that could no longer feel, and set his teeth, and said over and over again under his breath: I can't stop it. I can't stop it. There is nothing I can do.

③ Read the following passage:

There was once a woman who lived on the Russian side of the border between Poland and Russia. One morning, there was a knock on the door. It was the postman, telling the woman that the border between the two countries had been changed and that consequently the woman now lived in Poland. "Thank heavens," the woman said. "I don't think I could stand another one of those Russian winters."

On your own, write down your answers to these questions:

— The border has changed. How will this affect the weather?
— Where would she rather live? How do we know this? Write down what you think the woman's comments tell us about her feelings towards the two countries.

Further work

④ What we think about language can tell us about ourselves and our prejudices. Copy this table and then talk to people (friends, teachers, and relatives) and ask them to give you three examples of words or expressions they particularly love and hate. Some typical examples have been included below.

	Language they hate	**Language they love**
My teacher	Words such as 'nice'.	
My mum/dad		When I speak politely.
My best friend	Lists of spellings!	

⑤ Here is a list of 'language uses'. Write them out in order of priority, with your favourite at the top:
  — listing your favourite football players
  — writing birthday cards
  — reading funny poems
  — telling corny jokes
  — watching adverts
  — reading comics
  — listing what you want for your birthday
  — reading a good story
  — writing your own story
  — keeping a diary
  — writing postcards on holiday
  — using maps
  — writing plays
  — reading the words of pop songs.

Stores of language

The world is constantly changing and language changes with it. New words enter our vocabulary from other languages, cultures, new ideas and new technologies. Sometimes people invent new words, sometimes words drop out of use because we don't need them in our everyday life. The way we use words also changes as we get older.

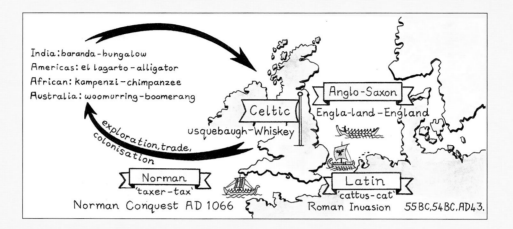

India: baranda - bungalow
Americas: el lagarto - alligator
African: kampenzi - chimpanzee
Australia: woomurring - boomerang

Celtic
usquebaugh - Whiskey

exploration, trade, colonisation

Anglo-Saxon
Engla-land - England

Latin
'cattus - cat'
Roman Invasion 55 BC, 54 BC, AD43.

Norman
'taxer - tax'
Norman Conquest AD 1066

Tasks

  These ten Latin words below form familiar English words.
Write out the Latin words, then link them to their modern English equivalents.

LATIN				ENGLISH		

LATIN

angelus   candela   clericus   missa

diabolus   discipulus   hymnus

monasterium   nonna   papa

ENGLISH

angel   disciple   monastery

Pope   nun   devil   candle

hymn   cleric   mass

Make notes on any similarities you notice between the words.

  Some words are commonly used in the things we do. These can include, for example, music, film, food and technology. Copy out these columns and then in pairs find four extra words used in each of these activities:

Music	Film	Food	Technology
rap	blockbuster	poppadom	cyberspace

We all have a store of words, or a vocabulary. In different situations we use different vocabularies.

③ Read the following extract:

> from *Ballad of the Bikkly Boy*
>
> You'd love the words that Bikkly used,
> Though some were rather silly:
> He wanted *goo* (that was his juice);
> He'd dance till he was *giggy.*
>
> He had more special words he knew
> Like sandwiches were *sam-sams,*
> And when I took him up to bed
> His blanket was a *bam-bam.*
>
> And in the morning he'd arise
> And ask to have his *soc-socs,*
> Yet soon as we had put them on
> The Bikkly took them off-off.
>
> The *dit-dits* were his tasty biscuits,
> And *wah-wah* was his wabbit;
> The way he kept repeating sounds –
> Sounds – formed a dreadful habit.
>
> *James Sale*

The poem is about the difference between a child's and an adult's language.
In pairs, discuss:
– why the poet has used italics for certain words
– how the little boy speaks
– the effect this has on the narrator's use of language.

Further work

④ List the specialist vocabulary in the box below under the correct headings:

Church   Military   Football   School

aisle	tank	goal	shot	pew	book	board	coach	bible
chapter	verse	operation	attack	captain	vicar	class	gun	font
corner	retreat	homework	discipline	formation	reconnaissance			
	choir	supporters	detention					

Write down the words that could go under more than one heading.
Write two sentences in which you use the same words to talk about different things, for example:

Their centre-forward scored in the first attack.
They were badly wounded in the first attack by the Martians.

What is grammar?

> Grammar is a system of rules which we all share. These shared rules help us communicate. Without these rules we cannot properly understand each other.

Tasks

 Which countries do the flags stand for?

 What do the traffic light colours mean?

 The semaphore signals above contain the letters 'd', 'r', 'o' and 'w' – but in the correct order. What word do they make?
Draw the signals for 'w' and 'r'.

Now that you have thought about these methods of communication, copy out the grid and tick which boxes are relevant to each type.

	Information	Ideas	Feelings
Flags			
Traffic lights			
Semaphore			

> CALL ME BUT LOVE AND I'LL BE NEW BAPTISED.

 Write a paragraph explaining which of these two lovers is more likely to be successful and why.

Now look at the bank of words below.

he she it selection
no but pleased because
since had of not felt walked walk
likes smiled smiles is could was library
wanted Rebecca find good book the pretty
Joseph doppelganger young Susan adolescent
James' occasionally liked talking to to to go
talking casually the nearby while books cookery
where she modern few would quite a
though happily and thumb through
energetically searching recipe but
for a satisfying curious

List as many sentences from this as you can.
Underline your shortest and longest sentences. How many words do they each have?

 Think of codes other than flags, traffic lights and semaphore.
In groups, make a list of them, explaining what each code does and why it is important.

Further work

 Write down three things you have found out about grammar.

 Design a flag for your school. The colours and patterns you choose should say something about what your school is like.

 Now write up to 100 words describing the good things about your school and what you think of it.

Finish by writing a short comparison of the flag and your description. Which says more about the school?

Pronunciation

> *Our lungs, tongue, lips, mouth and nose make speech. Pronunciation is linked to where we live and the people around us. It is the way in which we say the words we choose to speak.*

Look at the diagram below:

The Organs of Speech

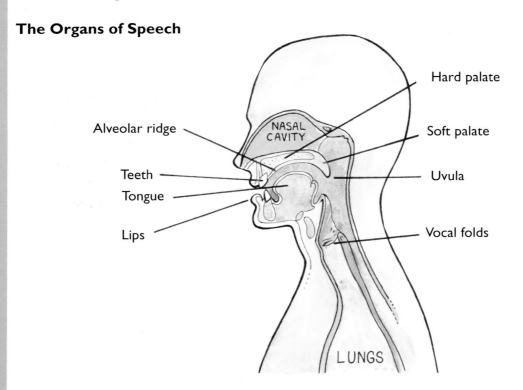

Try moving your tongue around your mouth: feel your teeth, the alveolar ridge, the hard and soft palate.

Tasks

 Working in small groups, take turns in reading these three extracts out loud as if you were reading them for a radio station. The first extract is an advertisement, the second is from a news report, and the third is from a music review programme.

> Oooh hello there, missus, Keefie Kettle here. And am I bunged up! Oh yes, it's all right for you, you don't care about limescale till it's floating around in your cup, but for us poor old kettles it's a different story altogether. What I need is 'Scale Off'. Cheap, clean and available from all good hardware stores and DIY centres. You'll never regret it. And neither will I, missus ...

The centre of Poole in Dorset is being evacuated tonight after a series of explosions rocked a chemical warehouse. Stephen Hall reports: The old town harbour area of Poole remains evacuated tonight. Police, fire officials and company chiefs still haven't been able to establish how toxic the cocktail of chemicals is that erupted here in three massive explosions just after six-thirty. The blast knocked two old people off their feet and hurled dozens of forty-gallon chemical drums into the air. One drum hit a car and incinerated it. Police, fire, and ambulance crews will be here for most of the night.
Stephen Hall, IRN, Poole.

And did that little exdoowopperdoo sound have you just rocking round your lounge tonight? Yes and we'll be taking a taste any minute now of a track from Bobbie Moore and the Rhythm Aces, who had some fine sides out on Chequer and this particular one is one to remember. This is me, Mike James, and you're tuned in to me and the Soul Hour with a shot of rhythm and blues and just stay with me for more good soul sounds right after the break ...

 Discuss:
 – how your pronunciation changed with each extract
 – why these changes occurred.

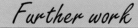

 On your own, say 'look', 'follow' and 'hill'. Your tongue will be in a slightly different position when you make the 'l' sound of each word.

Experiment with the sounds you can make with your tongue and your lips in different positions. Say the following words slowly and carefully, paying close attention to how your tongue and your lips are moving:

buttercup   freckle   toothbrush   structure   pretend   herself

drastic   grumpy   marble   restless   lipstick   crystal

 Choose any three words and write a description of how your lips and tongue move as you say the words.

Vowels and consonants

> There are 26 letters in the English alphabet. Of these, five are used to stand for vowels (a, e, i, o, u). The remaining 21 letters are called consonants. The five vowels are all made by using what is called an 'open' mouth (which means that we don't use our lips to stop the sound). The consonants are made by holding back or 'stopping' the sound for a while by, for example, closing our lips, and then quite suddenly releasing it .

Try this yourself by saying the word 'pop'. The first and the last letters are consonants (the letter 'p'), while the middle letter is a vowel (the letter 'o'). Say the word sound by sound, and you will see how the consonant is like a miniature explosion (indeed, the letter 'p' is called a 'plosive' sound, which means 'explosive'), while the vowel sound is made using an open mouth.

Tasks

 1 Copy out this chart. Pick out the vowels and consonants from the words on the left and copy them into the next two columns.

Word	Vowels	Consonants
blackbird	a, i	blckbrd
clumsy		
standard		
display		
peep		
trust		
control		
frighten		
toothpaste		
lipstick		

'Peep', as well as having two vowels and two consonants, is also a palindrome (a word that is spelt the same backwards or forwards).

 2 Write down which of these words are real palindromes:

level   **bad**   **noon**   **dead**   **poop**

repeater   **deified**   **deed**   **stoops**   **madam**

 3 Anagrams are words whose letters can spell another word (or words). For example, the letters of 'hated' also spell 'death'.

Write out anagrams for these words:

heart   **lisps**   **meaty**   **miles**   **nails**   **ought**   **panel**   **quite**

4 Secret codes let people share information without an outsider understanding what they are talking about. Groups develop ways of moving vowels and consonants about to make their own 'back-slang' language.

Look at this code carefully:

b	c	d	f	g	h	j	k	l	m	a	e	i
n	p	q	r	s	t	v	w	x	y	z	o	u

Using this substitution code, 'hello' becomes 'toxxe'. Look at the chart: h=t, e=o, l=x, o=e.

'I would like a cup of tea' becomes: **'u keixq xuwo z pic er hoz'**.

Discuss in pairs how this code has been made.
Now, in pairs, write out the following words and phrases using the code above:
— I have not done my homework.
— It is raining.
— My name is ...

Further work

 5 Create your own secret code by switching the alphabet letters around. Write a secret message.

 6 Write a brief account of a back-slang language you have heard and how it works.

Syllables

> *A syllable is a complete sound that contains one vowel, pronounced as a word or as part of a word. The word 'she', for example, has one syllable; 'to | mor | row' has three. The sentence 'Just go a | way' has four. Remember when you are looking at syllables to think about sounds, not necessarily letters. 'Chocolate' has three syllables if we pronounce it 'cho | co | late', but two syllables if we say it as most people say it: 'choc | late'.*

Tasks

 1 Separate your first name into syllables. If you have a name like 'John' it will be easy ('John' is one syllable). But how many syllables would 'Johnny' or 'Jonathon' have? Or 'Elizabeth' – this could be 'Liz', 'Beth', 'Lizzy' or 'Libby'. How many syllables do each of these names have?

In pairs, write down the longest (in terms of syllable count) male and female names that you can think of.

 2 The poem below is called a **cinquain**. How many syllables are there in it?

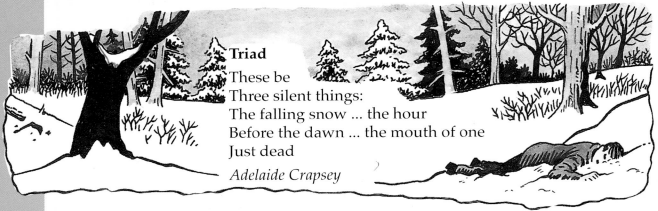

Triad

These be
Three silent things:
The falling snow ... the hour
Before the dawn ... the mouth of one
Just dead

Adelaide Crapsey

 3 Now look carefully at the cinquain and write out its syllable pattern and how many syllables there are in each line. Discuss the point of the short last line.

 4 Write down:
- five words of **one** syllable
- five words of **two** syllables
- five words of **three** syllables.

Mark where one syllable ends and another begins with a straight vertical line.

 5 Write down as many words you can think of that have more than four syllables. Note which of these words has the most syllables.

Stress

> *Stress is when one syllable in a word is emphasised. You can hear emphasis in your voice – your voice 'rises' when a syllable is stressed. For example, 'hello' has two syllables: 'hel/lo'. The second syllable has more emphasis than the first.*

 6 When you want to show which syllable is stressed, you mark it with a rising line:

morning – the voice is rising (see large bold stroke).

The other syllable is pronounced but not stressed in the same way. We call this unstressed and we write it:

morning – the voice is dipping (see large bold ‿).

 7 Copy out the table below containing words of one (mono-), two (bi-) and three (tri-) syllables. The first line is done for you. Words of one syllable will be stressed. Complete the stress markings for the other words.

Monosyllabic		Bisyllabic		Trisyllabic	
to		today	‿ ´ today	tomorrow	‿ ´ ‿ tomorrow
in		insert		interrupt	
for		forward		forefinger	
a		abode		aniseed	
out		outdoor		outsider	

Further work

 8 Copy out this sentence:

It is <u>to-night</u> in Donkey Street, <u>trotting</u> <u>silent</u>, with seaweed on its <u>hooves</u>, <u>along</u> <u>cockled</u> <u>cobbles</u>, past <u>curtained</u> <u>fernpot</u>, text and trinket, harmonium, holy dresser, watercolours done by hand, <u>china</u> dog and rosy tin teacaddy.

Mark the stress pattern on all the underlined words.

Circle all the words of more than one syllable in the sentence.

Intonation

Intonation is a way of emphasising a word or several words in a sentence.

Tasks

Working in small groups, imagine the following:

Suppose you have been waiting to meet some friends and they are late. When they finally arrive, you might greet them with the words: "I'm so glad you got here at last." But how you say the words, how and where you pause, where you place emphasis in the sentence – your intonation – can easily change the meaning of your greeting.

 Say the sentence in turn, emphasising the word or phrase in capitals. Give a slightly different meaning each time.

I'M so glad you got here at last.

I'm so glad YOU got here at last.

I'm so glad you GOT here at last.

I'm SO glad you got here at last.

I'm so glad you got HERE at last.

I'm so GLAD you got here at last.

I'm so glad you got here AT LAST.

 Discuss with the rest of the group what they thought you were 'really' saying from the way you greeted them:
– Were you being sarcastic?
– Were you genuinely pleased that they had indeed arrived safely?
– Have you entirely forgiven them all for having kept you waiting for so long?

 One famous example of a speech where intonation is important is when Macbeth (in Shakespeare's play) worries about plotting to murder his king because of possible failure.

He says: **'If we should fail?'**

His wife, Lady Macbeth replies, quite simply: **'We fail.'**

Working in pairs, rehearse these two lines:
– How many ways can you say **'We fail'** and how does it change the meaning?
– Write a short paragraph explaining three possible differences in meaning.

Rhythm

> **Rhythm is the movement of stressed and unstressed sounds in a sentence.**

Tasks

The best way to find rhythm is to hear it.

 1 In pairs, read this poem aloud. Clap your hands to what you think is the rhythm of the poem.

My auntie had a baby
And she called him tiny Tim, Tim, Tim.
She put him in a bucket
To see if he could swim, swim, swim.

He swallowed a gallon of water,
He swallowed a bar of soap, soap, soap.
He tried to swallow the bucket
But it wouldn't go down his throat, throat, throat.

Operation said the doctor,
Operation said the nurse, nurse, nurse.
Operation said the lady
With the alligator purse, purse, purse.

James Sale

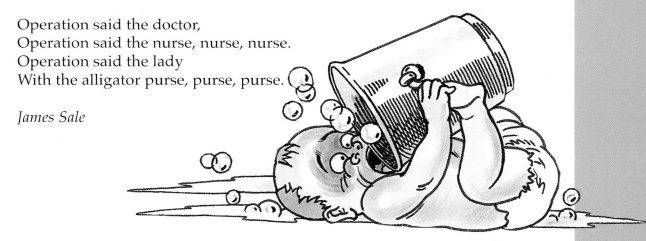

2 Copy the poem. Working with your partner, underline where the stresses occur.

Further work

 3 Write down the words of your favourite pop song.

 4 Underline the words for stresses.

 5 Write a paragraph explaining why certain words or patterns of words are stressed.

Rhyme

Words are linked in different ways; sometimes by sound, sometimes by their meaning and look. Rhyme is the repetition of the same sound in two words. For example, 'love' rhymes with 'dove'.

Two lines together which rhyme are called a couplet:
> God created the little fly
> And then forgot to tell us why!

Tasks

 1 Here are some first lines. Copy out and complete the couplets:

I knew what noses were for

_____

She met him in a darkened hall

_____

There once was a man who lived up a pole

_____

Oh, my, it's terribly sad

_____

He spoke politely, "How do you do?"

_____

 2 Copy out this rhyme page; you can add to it to make a book. You will find it useful when writing rhyming poems.

Pets	rhyming word	Family	rhyming word	Sports	rhyming word
cat	hat	dad		ball	
dog		gran	can		
horse	racecourse				
snake					
fish					

Add as many words as you like to the subjects. Find words to rhyme with them. Remember, words that rhyme can have more than one syllable ('racecourse').

Further work

 3 Using your rhyme page, write a poem about pets, family or sport.

 4 Go through your poem and mark all the stressed words.

Roots

Many words in English come from other languages and often their meanings are similar to their meanings in the original language. Once they enter English these words can then change and develop. Quite soon we forget the original language.

For example, the familiar English word 'fortune' comes from the Latin 'fortuna'. 'Fortuna' means luck, usually good luck. We still use the word in this way in English, but sometimes it has a slightly different meaning. For example:

She has just won a fortune on the Lottery.

Tasks

 1 Discuss what the meaning of the word 'fortune' is in the example above.

2 Write down three other words that come from the word 'fortune'. The first has been done for you:

Fortune: **fortunate**

 3 Some words are so successful that many other words 'grow' from them. Look at the word 'natal'. In English this means 'birth'. It comes from the Latin word 'natalis' meaning 'to be born'.

	Natural
Natal:	**Native**
	Nation
	Nativity

Using a dictionary write down the meanings of these four words.

What part of the word links these words together?

Further work

 4 Copy out this table. For each of the following words find three other words that are related to them:

Real	**Sense**	**Human**
really	senseless	humane
realise		
unreal		
reality		

 5 Create your own store of words connected with the Lottery. These might include, for example, 'cash' and 'draw'. Write a brief television advert reminding people to watch the draw.

Dictionaries

> *A dictionary is a book that lists words and gives their meanings. Sometimes it shows how words are pronounced and where they come from.*

Tasks

 Dictionaries are extremely useful books, especially when we meet words we are not sure about. Read these sentences. Write out what you think the meaning of the underlined word is, then check in a dictionary.

- Her idea was <u>ingenious</u>.
- Her classroom behaviour was <u>reprehensible</u>.
- His running was <u>erratic</u>.
- My <u>condolences</u> to your father.
- The Minister's <u>sermon</u> was boring.
- She was extremely <u>candid</u>.
- His <u>forthright</u> manner won him many friends.
- The <u>suggestion</u> was not welcome.

 The first real dictionary of the English language was written by Dr Samuel Johnson and published in 1755. Even Dr Johnson occasionally made mistakes, or revealed his prejudices! Here are some of his words and definitions.

The final column is left blank – copy out the definition from your school dictionary. Write about the differences between Dr Johnson's and the modern definitions.

Word	Dr Johnson's Definition	School Dictionary Definition
oats	a grain, which in England is generally given to horses, but in Scotland supports the people	food for horses (difference – Dr Johnson's definition sounds insulting to Scots)
network	any thing reticulated or decussated, at equal distances, with interstices between the intersections	
pension	an allowance made to any one without an equivalent. In England it is generally understood to mean pay given to a state hireling for service to his country	
cough	a convulsion of the lungs, vellicated by some sharp serosity	
garble	to sift; to part; to separate the good from the bad	

3 Defining words can be a way of making an amusing point. Ambrose Bierce in his *Devil's Dictionary* defined a cat as 'A soft, indestructible automaton provided by nature to be kicked when things go wrong in the domestic circle'. Write an amusing definition of a dog.

 4 The *Hitch-Hikers Guide to the Galaxy* described Earth as 'harmless'!

Write descriptions for other planets in the solar system.

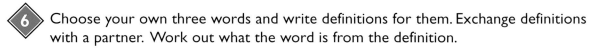

Further work and revision

 5 Write definitions for the following words:

mother   playground   pen   gossip   smile   pretty

6 Choose your own three words and write definitions for them. Exchange definitions with a partner. Work out what the word is from the definition.

7 Write down five words that rhyme with 'oats'.

8 Write a couplet using two of the words rhyming with 'oats'.

9 Write a whole poem using your couplet as the first two lines.

Thesauruses

A thesaurus is like a dictionary – it is a book of words. The difference is that the thesaurus supplies lists of words of similar meanings. Words of similar or like meaning are called synonyms. (Words of opposite meaning are called antonyms.)

For example, a synonym of 'wise' is 'intelligent' (an antonym of 'wise' is 'ignorant').

Tasks

 1 Discuss in a group any differences in meaning you notice between these three sentences:
- Mary is female.
- Mary is feminine.
- Mary is womanly.

 2 Remember, synonyms do not mean exactly the same thing. Look at these three sentences:
- The cat is female.
- The cat is feminine.
- The cat is womanly.

Discuss which of these sentences does not make much sense and why.

 3 Using a thesaurus (and its index) find synonyms for the following words:

beautiful   clever   mad   happy

 4 The antonym of 'female' is its opposite – 'male'. Copy and complete the following:

female   –   male

feminine

womanly

 5 One advantage of using a thesaurus is to prevent your writing from becoming dull. People say:

"That's a nice cup of tea."
"Oh, he's very nice."
"Nice weather we're having."
"It would be nice if you could pop round."
"I heard a nice song today."

Use a thesaurus to rewrite these sentences. Use alternatives for 'nice'.

 6 One antonym of 'nice' is 'nasty'. Rewrite the sentences substituting 'nasty' for 'nice'. Make a note of those sentences that still work; find synonyms for 'nasty' for those sentences that don't.

Further work and revision

 7 Note down at least two synonyms for these four words:

reckon   **share**   **weak**   **break**

List antonyms for these four words:

fair   **good**   **lazy**   **brave**

 8 Read the following sentence:

Mary's new computer was really great.

This sentence does not mean that the computer was huge or massive in size. Using a thesaurus, find the section for the word 'great' and write down which words you think could replace it in the sentence.

 9 Using a dictionary, look up and make notes on the words:

female   **feminine**   **womanly**

In your own words explain the differences in meaning.

Prefixes

A prefix comes at the beginning of a word and changes or adds to the meaning of the word. The prefix 'dis' at the beginning of 'dislike' changes the meaning of the word 'like' to its opposite.

It is useful to know about prefixes because they can help you to understand what a word means and how to spell it. Look at this:

'**Natal**' means '**birth**'.
'**Ante**' means '**before**'.

Therefore, '**antenatal**' means '**before birth**'.

The prefix which is opposite to 'ante' is 'post'. This prefix means 'after' or 'following'. Write down what 'post-natal' means.

Tasks

 Copy out these words and write down their meanings. Write down what the prefixes (underlined) mean.

<u>post</u>mortem   <u>homo</u>phone   <u>pro</u>noun   <u>super</u>natural

<u>tri</u>pod   <u>un</u>happy   <u>semi</u>circle   <u>amphi</u>theatre

<u>out</u>law   <u>peri</u>meter   <u>bi</u>nocular   <u>subter</u>fuge

 All these words use the same prefix. Copy these drawings. Label them and explain why they have the same prefix.

3 Choose four of the words from Task 1 and write down three more examples for each which use the same prefix.

 4 Many English place names have prefixes that tell us something about them:

Prefix	Meaning	Example
bourne/burn	stream	Bournemouth
mer/mar	lake	Margate
strat/stret/streat	street	Stratford
wick	dwelling or farm	Wickhampton

Here are three more frequently used prefixes:

glen   ham   pol

Find out what they mean. Give examples of place names that use them.

Revision

 5 Using a thesaurus, find three synonyms for each of the following words:

outlaw   supernatural   subterfuge

Write a sentence for each word that shows how it is used.

Suffixes

> *Many words have suffixes. Suffixes come at the end of words. One of the most common suffixes in English is 'ful' – as in beautiful, joyful, hopeful. This suffix is really the word 'full' with the second letter 'l' left off. So 'beautiful' means 'full of beauty'; 'joyful' means 'full of joy'; 'hopeful' means 'full of hope'.*

Tasks

 Copy out this table and find words to fill in the spaces:

-ful	-ry	-able	-ship	-ee
beauti-ful	carpent-ry	port-able	dictator-ship	refug-ee
joy-ful	dentist-ry	laugh-able	companion-ship	train-ee
hope-ful	infant-ry			

 One suffix can be added to another suffix to change the word still further. Look at these:

beauty	**beauty + ful = beautiful**	**+ 'ly' = beautifully**
joy	**joy + ful = joyful**	**+ 'ly' = joyfully**
hope	**hope + ful = hopeful**	**+ 'ly' = hopefully**

Write down ten other words ending in the suffix 'ly'.

The pictures below represent five jobs ending in the suffix 'or'. Write them down and add five more of your own.

3 Look at the tree below. At its base are some word stems or roots.
You can see that 'luck' makes 'lucky' if you add the suffix 'y'.

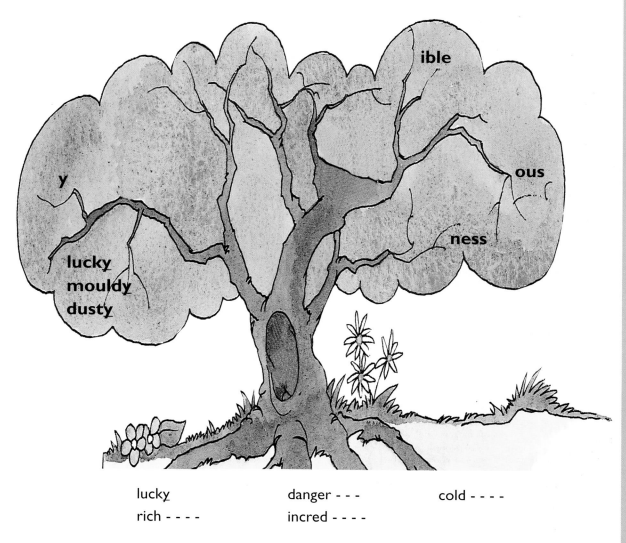

lucky   danger - - -   cold - - - -

rich - - - -   incred - - - -

Now copy the stems down and then for each of them add a suitable suffix from the branches of the tree. Then, find at least three other examples that share the same suffix. For example:

luck – lucky   **dirt – dirty**

mould – mouldy   **dust – dusty**

Further work

 4 Find a word ending in 'ful' which matches the following descriptions of people and write out the answers. The first letter is a clue:

– Someone who is shy: b - - - ful.

– Someone who is happy: c - - - - ful.

– Someone who is loyal: f - - - - ful.

– Someone who is nasty: h - - - ful.

– Someone who can't remember: f - - - - - ful.

Words-in-words

> *Suffixes help make new words. They also help us to compare things.*

For example: **John is mean.**

This is a statement about John. The word 'mean' describes John.

John is meaner than Sarah.

Here John's meanness is compared with Sarah's. The suffix 'er' has been added to the word 'mean'. By adding 'er' the word becomes comparative.

John is the meanest person I know.

Here John's meanness is beyond anyone else's. We call this the superlative. The suffix 'est' has been added to the word. This forms the word 'meanest'.

The pattern, then, is:

    mean
    mean-er
    mean-est

Tasks

 Complete the grid:

Word	Comparative	Superlative
tall	taller	tallest
	wetter	
		fittest
clever		
	stronger	

 Write out a sentence using each of the five words above in both their comparative and superlative forms. For example, 'John is taller than Sarah, but Mary is the tallest person I know'.

Not all words make the comparative or superlative by adding the 'er' and 'est' suffix. We cannot say 'John is horrider than Sarah', or 'John is the horridest person I know'. Instead, we use:
— The comparative (more ... than): 'John is more horrid than Sarah'.
— The superlative (most): 'John is the most horrid person I know'.

Some small but important words have a special comparative and superlative form. The best known is:

Word	**Comparative**	**Superlative**
good	better	best

 Copy and complete the following chart by using words from the box below.

Word	**Comparative**	**Superlative**
bad		
much		
few		

> **fewer   worse   fewest   worst   most   more**

 Read this short dialogue; look carefully at the comparatives and superlatives:

Steve: Give me a hand with this homework, Beth – you're much better at maths than me.
Beth: Better? You're joking! I'm the worst in the class.
Steve: What about that new boy, Omar, he got a lower mark than you in the test.
Beth: True. But you got the best mark in the class for the geometry section.
Steve: Yeah – but my overall mark was worse than yours. You were better than me and Omar.
Beth: Ok, Ok – but I'm no genius ... anyway, let's have a look ...
Steve: Here ... watch it! Aaarrgh! You clot! You've knocked ink all over it!
Beth: Sorry. I may not be the worst pupil at maths – but I'm definitely the clumsiest!

Answer the following questions:
— Who gained the highest score overall in the test?
— Who came last?
— Who came top in the geometry section?
— What superlative does Beth use to describe herself at the end?

Further work

 Write a paragraph that uses all of the following words in both their comparative and superlative forms:

happy   wicked   favourite   cheerful   weird

Spellings

English uses words from many different languages. The same spelling can have a different sound. There are patterns which are worth learning because they help your spelling. But remember: English has so many words, there are exceptions to most patterns.

Tasks

Common letter patterns: **ea gh ou qu**

  1 List four more words showing the pattern. Use the examples below to help you:

ea	(b<u>ea</u>d d<u>ea</u>d)	**gh**	(lau<u>gh</u> <u>gh</u>oul)
ou	(d<u>ou</u>ble t<u>ou</u>t)	**qu**	(<u>qu</u>een <u>qu</u>arrel)

  2 English spelling can be a problem. Two rules are especially helpful:

Rule 1
Read these two lists. In groups discuss any patterns you can see.

hop	hopping
rub	rubbing
hit	hitting
win	winning

sleep	sleeping
droop	drooping
groan	groaning
seat	seating

Write out what you think the spelling rule is.

Rule 2
Another common spelling pattern is 'i' followed by 'e', but also 'e' followed by 'i'.
A rule for remembering which way around the letters go is:
'i' before 'e' except after 'c'.

  3 Now look at these words. What is the rule for each list?

shriek	**receive**
piece	**ceiling**
friend	**deceive**
view	**conceit**
achieve	**receipt**

With most spelling rules there will always be exceptions. Use a dictionary and make a note of some of the exceptions. Here are some clues:

n - - ghbour	**prot - - n**	**spec - - s**	**s - - ze**
w - - ght	**v - - n**	**w - - rd**	**h - - ght**

Part Two

Choose two of the following:

 Write a cinquain about either Christmas, Easter, the summer or Bonfire Night. Your poem must have two syllables in the first line, four syllables in the second line, six syllables in the third line, eight syllables in the fourth line and two syllables in the fifth line.

 Write a speech praising someone you know, or someone famous, in which you use at least five comparatives and five superlatives.

 Write a paragraph describing a visit to your school by a group of your penfriends from a school in another country. You must include each of the following words at least once, making sure that you use and spell the words correctly:

their	site	board	of
there	know	write	lose
to	no	right	loose
two	weather	hear	quiet
too	whether	here	quite
sight	bored	off	

 Write a full-length story in which a dictionary – or thesaurus – is vital to the plot (what happens). The following are some suggestions you might wish to use:

— a girl on holiday with her parents discovers an old manuscript inside a book. It contains many difficult words, and needs to be deciphered.

— a friend of yours wants to send a letter to someone on Valentine's day, but he is no good with words. He asks you to write a flowery letter with lots of detailed words of praise. Write the story and include the faked letter.

— Lieutenant Loftus is on a trip to a new planet. When she gets there she meets aliens who speak a completely different language. Fortunately, one of them gives her a dictionary. Write the story of the trip including the Lieutenant using the dictionary.

Setting personal targets

 Look through the work you did in Section 2 and make a list of the things you did not understand or did not do very well. Keep your list to refer to.

 Talk to your teacher and choose at least three and no more than five of the following targets to meet. Make sure you choose both reading and writing targets. Use your list to help you choose.

Pronunciation

● I will look for opportunities to listen to people speaking. I will listen not so much to what they say, but to how they say it. Does pronunciation change when someone is in a different situation? For example, how does my best friend pronounce words when talking to:
 – me?
 – a teacher?
 I will keep a record of any interesting pronunciations.

Vowels and consonants

● I will make a list of palindromes I discover.
● I will choose a difficult word I have encountered in one of my curriculum subjects and I will try to make an anagram of it.
● I will write a letter to a friend in a secret code I/we have invented and shared. In it I will invite him/her to reply.

Syllables

● I will make a note of any syllable patterns I notice in the next poem I read.
● I will write three of my own cinquains.

Stress

● I will pick out an interesting paragraph from my reading book and study the words for their stress pattern. I will mark the pattern of each word in my exercise book.

Intonation

● I will spend half an hour trying to concentrate on intonation – how people say and emphasise certain words. Any words that have been spoken to me, which I think have been said in an unusual or striking way, I will jot down. I will ask the person who said them what they meant. I will write up my findings.
● I will go to the library and take out a play. Over the term I will read it. I will pay attention to the words and imagine how these might be spoken by actors and actresses.

Rhythm

- I will visit the library and look for poems that have a strong rhythm. I will make a list of the best ones. I will copy out my favourite and read it to friends, family, class or club.
- I will learn a poem by heart and recite it to the class.
- I will write a poem with a strong rhythm. I will mark the stresses and unstresses in the poem.

Rhyme

- I will write a poem using rhyme which describes the month. (For example, I will write an October poem.)
- I will write two poems that rhyme: one will rhyme in couplets and the other will not be in couplets (the rhymes will be spread out).
- I will go to the library and read as many rhyming poems as I can find. Whenever I find an interesting rhyme I will add it to my rhyme book.

Dictionaries

- Every time I meet a new word that I cannot work out in my reading I will use a dictionary to find its meaning.

Thesaurus

- I will use a thesaurus for any extended writing I do.

Spellings

- I will spend 10/20/30/40 minutes (choose) each week learning new spellings or correct spellings from words I have misspelled.

Sentences

Words need to be joined together to make sense. Joined together, they are called sentences. It is easy to recognise a sentence: it begins with a capital letter and it ends with a full stop and contains at least one verb.

Tasks

 Decide which of these are correct sentences:
- English is my favourite subject.
- A good pizza is delicious.
- a fine umbrella.
- red cockle shells in yellow syrup.
- wonderful weather
- I like pop music.

 Write six lines. Three lines should be correct sentences and three should not be sentences at all. Mark correct sentences with 'S' and the non-sentences with 'NS'.

Words in sentences have different jobs to do, like the human body. The body has different parts – brain, heart, lungs, liver, legs, fingers, and so on.

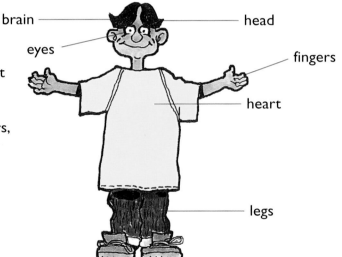

Each part of the body is useful. Some parts are essential – we could live without a finger, but not without a heart or a brain. The job of the heart is to pump blood to every part of the body. Words have 'jobs' to do in sentences – we call the jobs that the words do 'parts of speech'. Words doing different kinds of jobs are marked in this sentence:

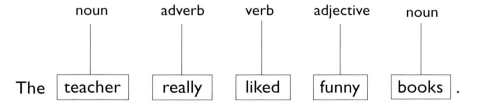

The [teacher] [really] [liked] [funny] [books].

noun — adverb — verb — adjective — noun

 Discuss in pairs which words in the sentence we could 'cut off' and yet still understand the sentence. Discuss which words are the most important.

4 Look at these sentences and put their words in a chart like the one below. The first is done for you:

- A cuddly pet is a great birthday present.
- Often I think hard about my dull homework.
- Some parents severely punish their children.
- My mother bakes the best cakes.

Quite important words	Very important words
a a	cuddly pet is great birthday present

5 You are a journalist. There is an incomplete message on your e-mail. Write out the message as a full sentence.

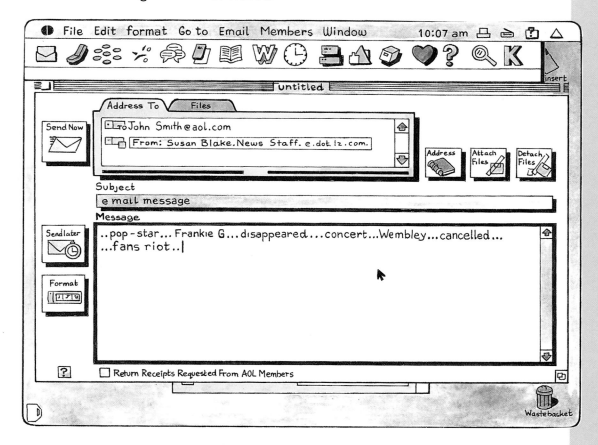

Further work

 6 Go through your exercise book and find the four longest sentences you have written. Identify the quite and very important words. Make notes on which words you find difficult to 'place' in the appropriate column, and why.

Common and proper nouns

> Nouns are a part of speech. Their special job is naming 'things'. There are common nouns and proper nouns.
>
> A common noun is a general name. A proper noun is a particular name and starts with a capital letter.

For example, the name we give to a young adult is either:

Common noun		**Proper noun**
a boy	but a particular name might be	Winston
or a girl	but a particular name might be	Amrit
We live in		
a town	but a particular name might be	Poole
or a city	but a particular name might be	Sunderland

Tasks

 1 Look at these words. Make a list of the common nouns:

bulb	mattress	beautiful	window	handsome
prettily	very	how	insect	person

 2 Go through your written work. Make a list of the five most frequently used common nouns.

 3 From the list below select and write out those words that are common nouns and those that are proper nouns:

pen	London	Susan	Mars
paper	teacher	brother	chocolate
Biro	Australia	Daz	liquorice
Henry Sugar	Teacher's Whisky	gun	Polperro
table	mum	rope	Macbeth

 4 Read the following sentences. Give capital letters to all the proper nouns:
- Hello! My name is jaspar and I've travelled all the way from delhi, via cairo and rome, to see you.
- shakespeare lived in stratford, but his plays were performed in london.
- amryl johnson, john betjeman, anne stevenson and brian hinton are all modern writers.
- william the conqueror conquered england nearly 1000 years ago.

5 There are two other occasions when a proper noun is used. The months of the year are always written with a capital letter: January, March, August.

Names of places often form other proper nouns: England – English, or America – American. The same is true of names: Margaret Thatcher's name led to the word Thatcherism. Shakespearean is a familiar word from a name.

Read this poem by a pupil who is confused by proper names and places:

If you're from Scotland – you're Scottish
You're English from England
Irish from Ireland ...
... they fit into place.

But Holland's not Hollish ...
Though Finnish is Finland ...
But Greenland's not Greenish ...
... I'm in a right old state!

Now, Scousers ... they're from Liverpool ...
And Cockneys from London ...
Brummies are from Birmingham
... I've learned them by heart.

But does that make Blousers from Blackpool?
And Swockneys from Swindon?
Does Gillingham make Grummies?
... No? I just can't work it out.

It's all too confusing – I'm leaving home soon ...
For a place where it's simple ...
I'll be a Loon on the Moon.

Chris Harris

6 Make a note of any other countries that fit the pattern (Scotland – Scottish). Scousers is not the 'official' name of people from Liverpool – they are called Liverpudlians. Write down the official names for people from London and Holland and any other countries or well-known cities.

Further work

7 The months of the year are often difficult to spell, especially the second and the ninth month. Write a sentence for each month of the year describing what you think is its most noticeable feature.

For example: **December is cold and rainy, but welcome because it's Christmas time.**

8 If people from England are called the 'English' write out what the people from these countries are known as: **Germany   Italy   France   Cyprus   Japan   Thailand**

Pronouns

> *A pronoun is a word that can be used in place of a noun. For example, 'he' instead of 'Michael'. Their job is to help you avoid having to repeat the same word.*

Look at the following:

The car has been scrapped. The car was in an accident.

This sounds clumsy because it repeats the word 'car'. If we use a pronoun to stand for the noun ('car'), things sound better:

The car has been scrapped. It was in an accident.

The pronoun 'it' stands for the noun 'car'. Look at the following sentence:

The car and the lorry have been scrapped. The car and the lorry were in an accident.

This becomes:

The car and the lorry have been scrapped. They were in an accident.

 Tasks

 Here are some pronouns:

it   she   their   we   they   her

Rewrite the following sentences replacing the nouns with the pronouns above. The nouns you need to replace are underlined.

– Rita was looking forward to being in the basketball team, but <u>Rita</u> broke her leg.

– Look at this watch. <u>This watch</u> belonged to my father.

– My neighbours go camping every year. This year <u>my neighbours</u> went camping in Scotland.

– I met Andy and Dean this afternoon and <u>Andy and Dean and I</u> went swimming.

– When you give the book back to Yasmin, ask <u>Yasmin</u> if I can borrow <u>the book</u> sometime.

– Linda and Errol were going to ride <u>Linda's and Errol's</u> bikes to the beach this morning, but <u>Linda's and Errol's bikes</u> both had punctures.

Sometimes poorly-placed pronouns lead to misunderstandings. Read the following passage carefully and see if you can work out who the murderer is:

Officer Trotter said he saw her climb in through Lord Fanshawe's window. Davies was in the garden at the time and rushed in to find them struggling. Trotter said she knew he was guilty because of the gun in his hand. She let Lady Fanshawe go when she realised it was a replica she had been holding. She returned outside, with Davies, to look for Lord Fanshawe's body which she found in the flower bed. Lord Fanshawe's son Barnaby told Trotter he had seen the whole thing from his study. Her companion confessed and was taken away.

Rewrite the story so that what happened is completely clear.

 Pronouns form a pattern:

I WE HE YOU THEY	ME US HIM YOU THEM
MINE OURS HIS YOURS THEIRS	MYSELF OURSELVES HIMSELF YOURSELF THEMSELVES

Write the beginning of a short story in which you use all of these pronouns.

Further work

 Look at the first paragraph of a non-fiction book. List all the pronouns used and the nouns to which they refer.

 'Which' and 'who' (or 'whom') are also pronouns. When are they used?

Collective nouns

> *A collective noun is a word that stands for a collection of like things – not just one thing.*

For example: person is a common noun but we need other words to represent several persons (collective nouns).

Here are three examples:

jury

committee

mob

As you read this now, you are probably in _____ , which is a collective noun. Write down the missing word.

Tasks

 Copy these words and underline those that are collective nouns:

books	nation
brothers	team
family	audience
flock	pencils
trips	people

 Many of the above collective nouns refer to people. Groups of animals can also have collective nouns. For example, wolves run in a pack.

List the collective nouns for these creatures:

lions	bees	fish	geese	cattle

3 The collective nouns underlined in this passage have been mixed up. Rewrite the passage with the collective nouns in the correct places, then continue the story using as many collective nouns as you can.

I was scuba-diving off the coast of America. I saw a <u>platoon</u> of beautiful fish swimming towards me. Too late I realised that they were fleeing from a <u>clump</u> of escaped outlaws trying to catch them from their raft. I swam to the shore and hid in the nearest field, by a <u>band</u> of trees, near a <u>swarm</u> of buffaloes. At that moment a <u>shoal</u> of soldiers came racing over the hill, chasing the escaped prisoners. At least, that's what I thought they were doing. In fact, they were escaping too! From a <u>herd</u> of bees!

4 A woman who was having a small operation had five doctors attending her. They popped in and out and each one had a very interesting opinion on her problem. There was only one nurse, and as the doctors came and went she made the woman comfortable, took her temperature, gave her a drink and got on with helping her.

The woman's husband – watching all this – finally said to the nurse: "What's the collective noun for all these doctors?"

Without hesitating she said, "A pain."

Invent an amusing collective noun for the following situations:

– A group of dentists around a patient's mouth.
– A group of anglers describing their catches.
– A group of golfers talking about their holes-in-one.
– A group of builders drinking tea outside a property they are working on.

Write down other interesting collective nouns you think appropriate for a particular situation.

Further work and revision

5 Write your own short tale leading to an amusing collective noun at the end.

6 Write out all the common nouns you can find in the four situations in Task 4.

Adjectives

> *An adjective tells us about the noun. Its job is to describe the noun. This is why adjectives are often called 'describing' words, because we use them to add description to something.*

The word 'door' is a noun. See how it grows by adding adjectives to it and how we gradually find out more information about the door:

The door.

The red door.

The big, red door.

The big, old, red door.

The big, old, battered, red door.

Adjectives make the writing more interesting and vivid.
They can be used to create a strong sense of atmosphere, character and setting.

To spot the adjective, simply ask yourself which word is telling us about the noun:

The red door – the noun is 'door'.
Ask yourself: 'What sort of a door?'
It is a **red** door – the adjective is the word '**red**'.

Tasks

 Write down the adjectives by answering the question following each of these sentences:

Example: **I saw a wild animal in my garden today.**
What was the animal?
The animal was **wild**. '**Wild**' is the adjective.

The restaurant has a Norwegian cook.
What sort of a cook does the restaurant have?

Every pupil will have Fridays off school in future.
What sort of pupil will have Fridays off school in future?

The fierce dog growled.
What sort of dog growled?

The grim-faced mourners filed past the coffin.
What sort of mourners are they?

There were five sweets in the bag.
How many sweets were there in the bag?

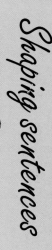

 Look at this sentence:

The fox jumped over the dog.

Here are some adjectives:

big   lazy   brown   tiny   smelly   tired

Add these adjectives to the sentence so that there is more and more information about the fox and the dog. Write down all the possibilities you can find.

 Here is another simple sentence: **The man met the woman.**

Write down at least ten adjectives that give more information about the man and the woman. For example:

The man is: happy   sad   young   old

The woman is:

 Here is a short poem that uses only adjectives. Read it and then discuss with a partner what well-known fairy-tale is being told.

> Excited, happy, child-like, free,
> Foolish, chatty, evil, sly,
> Cunning, hungry, nasty, bad,
> Suspicious, frightened, helpless, glad.

Further work

 Here is a piece of writing without any adjectives. Use your own adjectives to make this piece of writing as powerful and descriptive as possible. You can add whole sentences of your own, if you wish.

It is spring. There is a harbour with seagulls flying. A man is walking towards a boat. He is carrying some nets and buoys. There is the sound of a foghorn.

Verbs

A verb makes the action happen in a sentence. Its job is to link the parts of a sentence together. It is often the most important word in a sentence.

Tasks

 Read this sentence:

After dinner, he challenged Batman.

Now read these sentences:

– _____ dinner, he challenged Batman.
– After _____, he challenged Batman.
– After dinner, _____ challenged Batman.
– After dinner, he _____ Batman.
– After dinner, he challenged _____ .

In pairs, discuss how the missing word affects the meaning. Which word makes the most difference when it is missing? That word is the verb.

 With one word complete this sentence.

She _____ the football.

List as many words as you can to put in the sentence. Some of the words in your list may be unusual. But they will all be verbs.

 Now underline the five words in your list that are the most interesting. Use them to write five new sentences of your own.

 You may have verbs such as 'kicks' or 'kicked' in your list. 'Kicks' is present tense; 'kicked' is past tense. Whichever tense you have used in your five new sentences, now change them to the other tense. What letters normally show the past tense is being used?
Select a paragraph from any fiction book you are reading. Copy it out and underline every verb you can find.

5 Some words are singular and need the singular verb:

| anyone anybody everyone | IS | Is anyone there? Anybody is welcome. Everyone is happy. |

Some words are plural:

| many few both | ARE | Many are called. But few are chosen. Both are right. |

Write down these sentences and correct them as necessary:

— Are everyone going to school?

— If anyone are waiting for a lift I will take them.

— Both the soup and fresh bread is tasty.

— Many Second World War aeroplanes are now on the scrap heap.

— Few birds is nesting in this area.

Further work and revision

 6 Look at the nouns below. Add suitable verbs to them and write a short piece called *Street Morning*.

> traffic-lights
> baby in a pram
> clouds
> shopkeeper
> cyclist
> milk-bottles
> traffic-warden
> children
> tramp
> dog
> sun

 7 Write out the proper noun, common noun and pronoun from this sentence (in that order):

After dinner, he challenged Batman.

Adverbs

An adverb is a word whose job it is to describe verbs.

For example:
  He walks ... slowly.
  He walks ... strangely.
  He walks ... proudly.

How does he walk? The adverb describes the action of the verb 'walk'.

Tasks

 Here is a list of verbs and adverbs. Match adverbs with their most likely corresponding verbs – some may suit more than one verb.

Words	Verb	Adverb
talk fondly		
fight soundly		
love fiercely		
weep dearly		
hate sadly		
kiss clearly		
sleep passionately		
remember boldly		

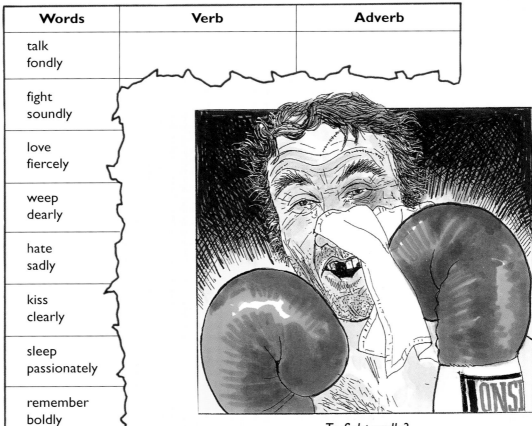

To fight sadly?

Write down what the spellings in the adverb column have in common.

 Often it is easy to form adverbs from adjectives:

He is slow at running. becomes **He runs slowly.**

52

© Folens

Write down the adverbs from these adjectives:

swift   cold   brave   beautiful   keen   fatal   soft   distinct

Now correctly use the eight adverbs formed in sentences of your own.

 Adverbs can describe the 'how' of a verb. They can also describe the 'when' and 'where'.

> He will talk ... **proudly**. (how)
> He will talk ... **tomorrow**. (when)
> He will talk ... **here**. (where)

Use the words in the box below to answer the following:

— 'Tomorrow' is an adverb telling us 'when' the action of the verb happens.
Write down at least two other possible words that can tell you 'when' something will happen.

— 'Here' is an adverb of 'where' the action of the verb happens. Write down at least two other possible words that can tell you 'where' something will happen.

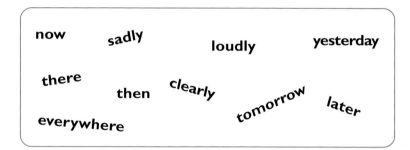

Now use each word in a sentence.

Further work

 Add verbs and adjectives to this list of nouns and adverbs to create an atmospheric ten-line poem:

owl	churchyard	oak tree	now
boy	weeds	swiftly	gravestone
wind	church tower	moon	softly

You could start:

A shadowy owl swiftly swoops ...

Subject and predicate

> *The subject and predicate make up a sentence. The link word is the verb. Find the verb, and then ask: 'who' or 'what' does the verb. The answer to this is the 'subject'. All the rest is the 'predicate'.*

'The man walked.'

Find the verb – 'walked'
Who does the verb? – 'the man.'

So, the man is the subject of the sentence, and the rest ('walked') is the predicate.

the man   **subject**
walked   **predicate**

the man
walked slowly

the old man
walked slowly

the old man
walked slowly up the hill

the poor old man
walked slowly up the hill towards the house

the poor old man and his friend
walked slowly up the hill towards the house

the poor old man and his friend
walked slowly up the hill towards the haunted house

MARSTYN HOUSE

FOR SALE
TEL
01324 557913

Tasks

I   Read these sentences and write out which parts are subject and which predicate on two lines as above.
   – The tree bends.
   – The sky roars at trees.
   – They shut the road through the woods.

– This wind brings all dead things to life.
– The sea is a hungry dog.
– From the steamed car's safety I see a dark land.
– At Flores in the Azores Sir Richard Grenville lay.

 Create a series of longer sentences (like 'the man walked' series) and divide the sentences into subject and predicate.

 Read this poem:

I Saw a Peacock with a Fiery Tail

I saw a peacock with a fiery tail
I saw a blazing comet drop down hail
I saw a cloud with ivy circled round
I saw a sturdy oak creep on the ground
I saw an insect swallow up a whale
I saw a raging sea brim full of ale
I saw a drinking glass sixteen foot deep
I saw a well full of men's tears that weep
I saw their eyes all in a flame of fire
I saw a house as big as the moon and higher
I saw the sun even in the midst of night
I saw the man that saw this wondrous sight

Anon

Discuss with a friend what is strange about the endings and beginnings of each line.

Remember, the predicate does not have to come after the subject.

Further work and revision

 Write your own 'predicate poem'. Start with a series of vivid descriptions. The predicate at the end of the line should fit with the start of the next line, for example:

I saw a vulture with a wicked smile
I saw a vampire...

 Go through the poem and identify **nouns**, **pronouns**, **adjectives** and **verbs**.

Capitals

> A capital letter is used at the beginning of a sentence. A capital letter is also called upper case, while a small letter is called lower case.
>
> Capitals or upper case: A   B   C   D   E   F   and so on.
>
> Small or lower case: a   b   c   d   e   f   and so on.

When to use a capital letter:

— When writing the personal pronoun 'I'.
— At the beginning of a sentence: It had been raining all day.
— For proper names: James, England, Wednesday, Paris, Italian.
— For the titles of films, books, plays, television programmes, poems and people (for example, *Romeo and Juliet*, *Eastenders*).
— For certain abbreviations: BBC (British Broadcasting Corporation).

Tasks

 Write out the following sentences, using capital letters correctly:

— george solomon has lived in and around canterbury in kent for many years.
— i'm planning to go to germany this summer with my wife, susan.
— mrs giddings bought an old porsche from the car auctions. she might have done better to have bought it from jenner's, the local porsche agent.
— david froggatt and jane slebbing were married at st george's church, merksham, near lincoln, last saturday.
— major losses were sustained by the british army during the first day of the battle of the somme.

 Now read this longer passage. Some of the capitals are in the wrong place – some are missing altogether.

peTer dawsoN knew the Moment He saw her that She was trouble. she was driving a ferrari and had just Gone through a Red Light when she almost knocked him dowN. Nothing like this had ever Happened before in little gidding. worse was to Follow. the mad woman leapt Out of her fancy Car and started swearing at him in french! peter could only Stutter ..."madam ... or is it ... miss ... don't You think ..." but before he could finish, She interrupted, in english.

"miss? madam? what are you saying you awful englishman! you may call me mademoiselle. mademoiselle lafayette!"

Rewrite the passage putting the capitals in the correct place.

 Folens

Words that can be removed entirely without changing the main point of a sentence should be marked off by commas.

 3 Copy out these five sentences and insert two commas correctly in each one:

- Westminster Abbey even though in the centre of one of the busiest cities is a beautiful building.
- The car although old completed its journey.
- John a ferocious bully was also a coward.
- To write a summary particularly of long books is difficult.
- My worst enemy unfortunately for me was myself.

Dear Granny,

Thankyou for your present I got a lot for Christmas. The presents I got were an action doll and a space gun and a tractor and a football and a computer game and sweets and a rocket science book and a bike and a deck of cards.

Love Joseph

 4 Rewrite the above letter using commas.

Further work

 5 Write instructions for one of the following activities using commas correctly. Include a list of the things you will need.

- Mending a puncture.
- Making a pizza/curry/cake – choose one.
- Creating and making an item of clothing.
- Dressing a wound, cut, bite or insect sting.
- Looking after a pet.

Speech punctuation

> There are special rules when writing down the actual words that someone speaks – when this happens it is called direct speech.

Remember: the actual words that someone speaks.

Look at these two sentences:
He said something about going to the cinema on Friday.
He said, "I am going to the cinema on Friday."

The first sentence reports something about what was said – it does not use the actual words. It is an ordinary sentence. The second sentence uses the exact words the speaker said. This needs special punctuation – speech punctuation.

- The actual words spoken are surrounded by speech marks ("..."). For example:
  "I have a dream."
- The speaker's words begin a sentence and so have a capital letter. For example:
  "Is that a lark I hear singing?"
- We need to know who said the words:
  Martin Luther King said, "I have a dream."
  Shelley said, "Is that a lark I hear singing?"
- Every new speaker starts a new line:
  Martin Luther King said, "I have a dream."
  Earlier, Shelley said, "Is that a lark I hear singing?"

Remember:

- Pronouns can be used instead of names: 'I', 'you', 'he', 'she', 'it', 'we', 'they' ... said.
- The 'who said' can come after the words spoken:
  "Is that a lark I hear singing?" said Shelley.

If 'said' comes before the quotation, there is a comma after it. If 'said' comes after the quotation, then the last word in the quotation has a comma (or other punctuation) after it.

Tasks

1 Look at these six sentences and turn them into direct speech. For example:
She said she liked music more than videos.
becomes
She said, "I like music more than videos."

- He said football was his favourite game.
- She said that April was the cruellest month.
- We said that we didn't like Mr Jones or his wife.
- John said that he didn't want to be form captain.
- Charlene said she was the best player in the school.
- Keats said that nightingales made him sneeze.

2 Discuss with a friend what the main rules for punctuating speech are.
Read the following passage and put in the correct speech mark punctuation.

I'll never go home again Tony said. It's murder living here. Well, you're not dead yet by the look of you Kylie said. You've a long way to go. But I can't escape – all the people wanting photographs and stories. Come on! don't be a wimp. You love it really. What would you do without it said Kylie. I'd find something said Tony. Bet you wouldn't said Kylie. Bet I would said Tony. Bet you wouldn't said Kylie. Bet I would said Tony. Bet you wouldn't said Kylie. Na-na-nee-na-na said Tony. That's being childish said Kylie. That's why I want to leave home said Tony.

 3 Repeating a word too often can make your writing dull and boring. Every time someone speaks we usually follow it with 'said ...'. If there are a lot of speakers the reader sees: 'said X ... said Y ... said Z' and so on.

Read this poem by Judith Nicholls.

Teacher Said

You can use
    mumbled and muttered,
    groaned, grumbled and uttered,
    professed, droned or stuttered
          ... but don't use SAID!

You can use
    rant or recite,
    yell, yodel or snort,
    bellow, murmur or moan,
    you can grunt or just groan
          ... but don't use SAID!

You can
    hum, howl and hail,
    scream, screech, shriek or bawl,
    squeak, snivel or squeal
    with a blood-curdling wail
          ... but don't use SAID!

          ... SAID my teacher.

Further work

 4 Judith Nicholls uses lots of words that communicate sounds. Use a thesaurus to find more. Make a list of them. If you are unsure of their meaning, or of any words in her poem, look them up in the dictionary.

Apostrophes

> *The apostrophe looks like a raised comma (') and is used to show either that one or more letters have been left out of a word (omitted), or to show that something belongs to somebody or to something (possession).*

Simply put the apostrophe (') where the letters have been missed out:

you will	can be shortened to ... **you'll**	('w' and 'i' have been left out)
I am	can be shortened to ... **I'm**	('a' has been left out)
they have	can be shortened to ... **they've**	('h' and 'a' have been left out)

 Tasks

 Copy out the box and fill in the gaps.

Phrase	Abbreviation	Letters missed out
you would	you'd	w, o, u, l
	they're	a
she has		h, a
	don't	
	we've	h, a
could not		o
		i
are not		

To show that something belongs to somebody or to something, follow these steps:

— First write the name of the owner: **Fred**
— Next add an apostrophe ('): **Fred'**
— And finally add an 's': **Fred's bike**.

Try it with your own name. Write your name, add an apostrophe, then add an 's'.

 Suppose you wanted to say something about your friend, Jane, who has beautiful hair. First, write the name of the owner of the hair:

— The owner of the hair is: **Jane**
— Next, add an apostrophe: **Jane'**
— And finally, add an 's': **Jane's hair**.

This shows that the hair belongs to Jane: **Jane's hair is really beautiful**.

3 Put an apostrophe in the right place in these sentences.
Follow the instructions on how to use the apostrophe.

For example:

The dog has a tail. So, we ask: **'To whom does the tail belong?'**

Answer: **The dog**.

So, we write: **The dog's tail**.

Now copy the table and try these sentences on your own.

Sentence	So we write ...
The girl has a book.	
The boy has a book.	
The men have guns.	
The women have daggers.	
The woman has a red Ferrari.	
The man has a Reliant Robin.	
The cat has fur.	
The cat has fleas.	
The flower has a scent.	
The flower has a stem.	

Shaping sentences

Further work

4 Rewrite the following passage, putting the apostrophes in the right places. Some of the apostrophes show that letters have been omitted, while others show possession.

That couples two children arent like other children. Theyve been so successful at school its amazing. The girls particularly clever. Id like to think Davids going to pass as many exams as shes passed. But I dont think theres much chance of that. Davids interest just isnt in school, thats all it boils down to.

Tests

The following two pages test you on some of the language skills and activities covered in Section 3.

 Write down which of the following are sentences. Add capitals, full-stops, exclamation or question marks where necessary.

go he

she hit him because he

close the door

he will become a good footballer, in time

they told him because he

he crashed my bike because the brakes were faulty

nobody answered

a super

what time is it

that book was

 Copy out the following table, then write each word in its correct column.

Words	Proper nouns	Common nouns
london		
tony blair		
cake		
doorstep		
mozart		
city		
welsh		
queen		
brick		
pot		
princess		
beach		
sea		
universe		
linda		
thursday		
february		
lobster		
seven		
princess anne		

Use a **pronoun** for the underlined words in the following paragraph:

I was planning to meet Sheila for lunch, but guessed that <u>Sheila</u> would probably be late. Tom and Pete had warned me that <u>Sheila</u> had been late when <u>Tom and Pete</u> had arranged to meet <u>Sheila</u> at the beach. The beach was a beautiful place to be, but even <u>the beach</u> was not a good place to be left waiting for Sheila, who would probably turn up three hours late (or more), claiming that <u>Sheila's</u> car had broken down. In the event, <u>Sheila</u> never turned up at all.

 Write out the following sentences. Underline the verb in each.

— The boy chewed the cake.
— Batman bit the bitter butter.
— The plane landed on the runway.
— He took the change from the waiter.
— The car came along the street towards me.

Now write out the sentences again, adding an adverb to each.

 Here is a shopping list. Some of the words need capitals and some do not. Write the list out correctly.

> **shopping list for saturday afternoon**
>
> heinz baked beans
>
> beefburgers
>
> eggs
>
> supalife batteries (exchange for those bought last september)
>
> spaghetti hoops
>
> kellogg's corn flakes
>
> wiltshire sausages
>
> guinness
>
> uht milk
>
> pasteurised milk
>
> cheese
>
> wensleydale cheese (for susan)

Longer assignments

The following assignments are based on what you have learned in Section 3. Part One contains two compulsory tasks, Part Two gives you a choice of several assignments.

Part One: Compulsory

 Read the following passage. Then copy out the table and write the underlined words in the correct boxes.

The <u>big red door opened easily</u>, so I went inside. A <u>clock chimed loudly</u>, just as my <u>bare foot touched</u> the <u>filthy carpet</u>. I <u>moved cautiously</u> and <u>quietly</u>. The <u>door slammed</u>. I <u>waited</u>, hardly daring to <u>breathe</u>. I <u>heard</u> the <u>clock</u> ticking, <u>slowly</u>, <u>purposefully</u>. It <u>sounded</u> like the dripping of a <u>tap</u>, somewhere in the <u>inky darkness</u>. A <u>hand</u> rested <u>gently</u> on my shoulder.

Noun	Adjective	Verb	Adverb
door	big, red	opened	easily

 The following simple sentences need to be put into a whole paragraph. Rewrite using commas, full-stops and pronouns where needed.

- Sean needed lots of things for the party.
- Sean needed drinks.
- Sean needed snacks.
- Sean needed a fancy-dress outfit.
- Sean needed new tapes to play.
- So, Sean went into town.
- Sean went to the supermarket.
- Sean went to LowPrice Records.
- Sean also went to the fancy-dress shop.
- Sean came home.

Part Two

Choose two of the following:

 1   You have recently visited two quite different seaside towns while on holiday. One was great fun, and you found lots of interesting things to do there. The other was exactly the opposite. Write a letter to a friend describing the two towns. Use as many powerful adjectives as you possibly can to create a vivid sense of both.

 2   Write a short story entitled 'The Mysterious Accident at Upton House'. This has to be an exciting piece of writing, with at least two characters. Use speech marks, full-stops, question and exclamation marks appropriately.

 3   Write a short story based on these four things. Use plenty of adjectives and verbs to describe the scene and what happens next.

The sky   **Aircraft**   **Out of control**   **Runway**

 4   You are the editor of the school magazine. Another pupil has sent in the beginning of a story he or she wrote for homework asking for advice on how to improve it.

Rewrite it, adding:

- adverbs
- adjectives
- commas
- pronouns.

> I was on the bus on the way to school. The bus was slow and dirty and packed full of pupils. Pupils were everywhere.
>
>   A man stood up. I grabbed his place. I looked out of the window. It was raining. Suddenly, a boy spoke to me. The boy told me to move. I refused. He clutched me with his hands, but luckily my friend Oscar was nearby. Oscar was a good friend and often came to my rescue.

Setting personal targets

 Look through the work you did in Section 3 and make a list of the things you did not understand or did not do very well. Keep your list to refer to.

 Talk to your teacher and choose at least three and no more than five of the following targets to meet. Make sure you choose both reading and writing targets. Use your list to help you choose.

Sentences

● I will check my written work to make sure every sentence is complete.
● I will test myself on what the various parts of speech mean (noun, verb and so on).

Common, proper and collective nouns

● I will go through my English work and check that all proper nouns begin with capital letters.
● I will keep a checklist of all collective nouns I meet in my reading or speaking and I will try to use them in my writing.

Pronouns

● I will visit the school library and copy out one/two/three short poems. I will underline all pronouns.

Adjectives

● I will consider a range of adjectives when describing something/someone in a story – not just the first ones that come into my head.
● In my next story I will use at least 20/30/40 different adjectives.

Verbs

● I will find a poem or story in which verbs are used in a striking way. I will make a note of which verbs and why I think they are striking.

Adverbs

● In my next piece of creative writing I will use at least ten different adverbs.

Capitals

● I will go through my work book and check I have used capital letters correctly and appropriately.
● I will make sure every sentence I write begins with a capital letter and ends with a full-stop (or question mark or exclamation mark).

Ending a sentence

- I will use question marks and exclamation marks to improve meaning.
- I will check my use of question marks – especially in written conversation/speech.
- I will check all commas I use to make sure that they shouldn't be replaced by full-stops.

Commas

- I will use commas in lists correctly.
- I will use commas to separate information in a sentence.

Speech punctuation

- In my next story I am going to have at least two characters who speak to each other, and I will use speech marks appropriately.
- I will check I have used a new line for each speaker.
- I will check I have put punctuation inside speech marks, where appropriate.
- I will check I have used alternatives to 'said'.

Apostrophes

- Every time I see an apostrophe in my fiction reading I will decide whether it is being used to show possession or omission.
- I will identify the three most common errors I make when using the apostrophe for omission. I will try to stop myself making those same three mistakes.

Titles

A title is the name given to a piece of work. It helps identify it. It helps us understand what the work is about – providing a vital clue. It can even add to the meaning of the work.

Read the following poem on your own:

I saw her
I saw her in the square
I saw her bleeding in the square
I saw her staggering in the square
I saw her being killed in the square
I saw her ... I saw her ...
And when he shouted
Who is her guardian?
I denied knowing her
I left her in the square
I left her bleeding in the square
I left her staggering in the square
I left her dying in the square
I left her ...

Samih al-Qasim

Tasks

 In pairs, discuss what you think the best title for this poem might be:

I Saw Her   **The Square**   **Abandoning**

I Left Her   **Fear**   **In the Square**   **Guilt**

2 Write down five new titles of your own and put them in order with the best one at the top.

3 A famous riddle:

Four and twenty white bulls
Sat upon a stall,
Forth came the red bull
And licked them all.

A title would give the game away. Discuss with a friend what it might be.

4 Write a paragraph on each of these titles saying what you think the stories are about:

- The Eighteenth Emergency
- The Lost Heart
- The Go-Between

5 Hours, days – perhaps even weeks or months – are often spent choosing titles for books, songs, magazines and so on. Listed below are three texts that need titles. In a small group read the descriptions:

A new magazine

For teenagers. About football. Lots of gossip and unusual facts. Lots of pictures of the biggest stars. Letters from fans. Glossy but thin.

A new 'serious' newspaper (for Sunday)

Rather old-fashioned look. Not many pictures. Black and white. Respectable. Lots on business and politics.

A new horror novel

Set in Australia. Has a vampire-kangaroo terrorising a small town in the outback. Kelly Hunter, a local schoolgirl, sets off to track down the creature.

Taking each subject in turn, brainstorm or list as many possible titles for each, making sure they fit the subject and catch the attention. Then, in your group, cast votes for each until you have your three choices. On your own, write a short paragraph for each title, saying why it was your group's choice.

Revision

6 List all the verbs in Samih al-Qasim's poem.

Sentences, paragraphs and whole texts

Words joined together make sentences. Sentences joined together form paragraphs. Paragraphs link information, ideas and emotions together. Paragraphs linked together make the whole text – the complete work.

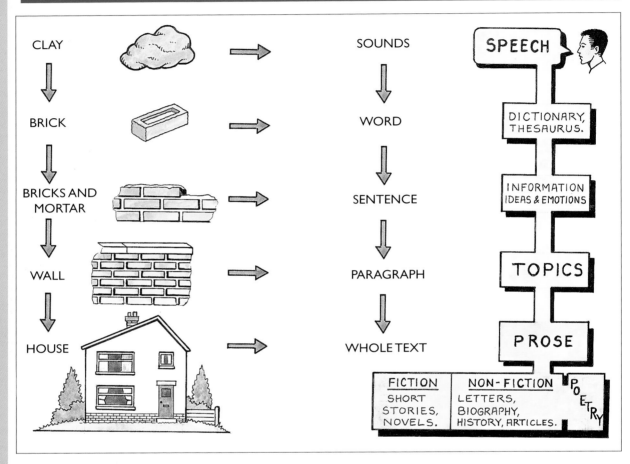

Language is like building blocks – small blocks build into bigger blocks.

Tasks

 Look at these three jumbled piles of words – make three sentences from them and write them down:

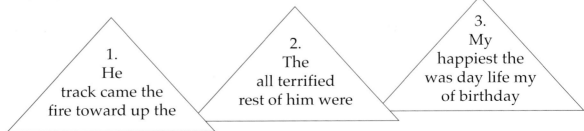

1.
He track came the fire toward up the

2.
The all terrified rest of him were

3.
My happiest the was day life my of birthday

Like bricks, language must be put together in useful patterns.

In handwritten work the new paragraph is shown by indenting the line:

This paragraph is neatly indented, about 4mm from the edge of the page. Perfect.

In typed work new paragraphs are not always indented:

I am typing this sentence but I am not indenting it, although it begins the paragraph.

Now read this:

A short paragraph will contain just one or two ideas. It does not need to develop ideas at length and so can be quite brief.

When we write longer paragraphs it is because we need to explore more complicated thoughts. Longer paragraphs let the writer bring in extra information and show the reader that the topic is being more fully discussed. It is important in reading longer paragraphs to pick out the key idea or ideas. Usually, there are one or two sentences that have this information.

 2 Read this extract. Copy it out and show where each new paragraph begins. There are three paragraphs.

She found her soft-sided suitcase where she'd left it by the door and lifted it with her left hand. The bag was heavy, filled with a week's worth of clothes. Kelly leaned far to the right as she opened the door and staggered into the hallway. Her skis and ski pole were waiting at the top of the stairs. The skis were several inches longer than Kelly was tall. Getting them balanced across her shoulder was quite a trick. The combination of heavy bag and lengthy skis made her wobble as she walked down the hallway, the tips of her skis drawing figure-eights in the air. As she turned to go down the stairs, the skis cracked loudly against the wall. Kelly cringed. She stopped, waiting to see if there was any reaction. When no one stirred, she started down again. Two steps later, the skis hit the wall a second time. After that, Kelly took the steps very, very slowly.

 3 Write three more paragraphs to add to this short extract. Try to write at least one short and one longer paragraph.

Further work

 4 Write a complete short story based on your ideas of what you think happens.

Chapters and verses

> *A chapter is a main part of a whole story or book. It is big enough to be given a title, although chapters may simply be called Chapter One, Chapter Two, Chapter Three and so on.*

Here is the outline of the first six chapters of *Animal Farm*, a novel by George Orwell.

When Mr Jones is asleep, all his animals on Manor Farm meet in the barn. Major, a pig, recounts his dream of freedom. All the animals are excited by it, but their noise wakes Mr Jones. He shoots his gun. They rush back to sleep. Major dies. Shortly after, due to Mr Jones' mistreatment of the animals, Napoleon and Snowball, two pigs, lead a rebellion. They throw Mr Jones off the farm and set up their own government. They call it Animal Farm and it has its own rules. They want all animals to be equal. The animals are happy working for themselves, but the two leaders, Napoleon and Snowball, have different ideas about how to lead the farm. However, the pigs all appear to have extra privileges. Mr Jones tries to win back his lost farm by force. His attack is met bravely by the animals and he is beaten. Snowball shows particular courage. There is much rejoicing on Animal Farm. One of the animals leaves, not happy with the shared hardships of the farm. Increasingly, bitterness is shown between Napoleon and Snowball. Napoleon trains dogs, and these attack Snowball – who only just escapes. Napoleon takes control of the farm. The animals work really hard. Napoleon starts trading with humans, despite this being against Animal Farm rules. Squealer, another pig, explains to the other animals there is no contradiction. The pigs start living in Mr Jones' house. A windmill is blown down and Napoleon blames Snowball.

Tasks

 The first chapter has been fitted into the first box. Copy out the boxes and do the same for chapters two to six. Each chapter should introduce a new part of the story.

Chapter One: When Mr Jones is asleep, all his animals on Manor Farm meet in the barn. Major, a pig, recounts his dream of freedom. All the animals are excited by it, but their noise wakes Mr Jones. He shoots his gun. They rush back to sleep.	**Chapter Two:**	**Chapter Three:**
Chapter Four:	**Chapter Five:**	**Chapter Six:**

2 Here are ten chapter titles from a horror novel. List them in the most likely order:

- Through the Woods
- A Very Heavy Anchor
- A Chase in the Dark
- Rats and Bats
- The Old Barge
- No Barge, No Body
- A Friendly Face
- Going for Help
- Midnight Breakdown
- Return to the River

Once you've sorted out your structure, exchange your chapter order with a friend. Take it in turns to tell a story based on the chapters.

 3 A verse is a number of lines of poetry that are not divided by a space. Often there are four lines to a verse.

> **Till in a gap of hazel glen –**
> **And not a hare in sight –**
> **Out lepped the nine-and-twenty lads**
> **Along his left and right.**

Look carefully at which words rhyme and how many syllables there are in each line. Here is some more from the same poem. Make three verses (four lines for each verse) from these words:

Then Danny smashed the nose on Byrne, he split the lips on three, and bit across the right-hand thumb on one Red Shawn Magee. But seven tripped him up behind, and seven kicked before, and seven squeezed around his throat till Danny kicked no more. Then some destroyed him with their heels, some tramped him in the mud, some stole his purse and timber pipe, and some washed off his blood.

Further work

 4 Reread the outline of the first six chapters of *Animal Farm*. Write down your own titles for each chapter, or write your own horror story based on the chapter titles in Task 2.

Openings

> *A good opening to a story describes a person or a place in an interesting way. It is important that the opening grabs our attention and makes us want to find out what happens and why.*

This is the opening to *Brighton Rock*, a novel by Graham Greene.

Hale knew, before he had been in Brighton three hours, that they meant to murder him.

We are given several facts in the first sentence about the character and the setting of the story. The character is called Hale; he is in Brighton. We are also presented with some unexplained details that heighten our interest – Hale knows that someone wants to murder him. Our attention is grabbed by the unspoken questions: Who wants to murder him? When? Why?

Tasks

 Eric Wright, a famous footballer, is just about to accept the FA Cup as captain of the winning team, and goal scorer. Write five possible opening sentences to this story.

 Read these two extracts which are both openings to famous novels:

> I will begin the story of my adventures with a certain morning early in the month of June, 1751, when I took the key for the last time out of the door of my father's house.
>
> *Kidnapped*, Robert Louis Stevenson

> I was born in the year 1632 in the city of York of a good family, though not of that county, my father being from Bremen in Germany, who had settled first at Hull.
>
> *Robinson Crusoe*, Daniel Defoe

Make a list of the things the passages have in common. Using your list, write your own opening to a novel telling your own story (for any character, at any time).

3 Obviously, stories begin in all sorts of other ways too. Read this opening carefully:

Why had she done it? Why hadn't she just walked away and carried on back up the road to her neat little house with its prim patch of lawn? She would never know. Her mind raced back to that moment – that moment when she'd stopped, reached into her handbag, and dropped a couple of coins into the tramp's filthy hand. After all, she didn't believe in charity. But that was then. Things were different now ...

Write down how this opening is different from the two by Defoe and Stevenson.
Copy out the particular sentences that make you want to read on.
Make notes predicting how you think the story will continue.

Further work and revision

 4 Write an interesting opening sentence for each of these subjects (not all of them come from novels):
- near miss at speed
- floral arrangements for beginners
- holiday adventure by the sea
- accident at home
- organising stamp collections
- the fight.

 5 Write out each of the above as titles, using capital letters where appropriate.

Closings

> *A good closing to a story makes us feel satisfied. The people and events in the story have reached an appropriate ending. However, it isn't always easy to find original endings.*

Tasks

 Read the following endings of stories written by school pupils:

she woke up. It had all been a dream.

Safe! He was safe at last!

and they lived happily ever after.

as a reward, the police gave me lots of money.

In a group, discuss these questions:

– Have you written stories that have finished in a way similar to these?
– What's wrong with the endings above, if anything?
– Are there other typical endings you know?
– What is the most surprising ending to a story you've heard, read or seen?

 In the novel *Hush-a-bye* by Susan Moody the character Harriet thinks she has lost her mother, and nearly loses her daughter. But her mother, at the end, suddenly appears to protect her. This is the last paragraph of the book:

Standing on the edge of the sea, feet steady on the slippery black rocks, Tom's arm in hers as they watched the coldly heaving water and, far out, the black head of seals, hearing the voices of her family about her, Harriet thought again of the mother distanced from her not only by place but by inclination, and told herself that perhaps next time the telephone rang and no one spoke, she would speak herself, she would talk gently of Laura, of Matthew, of Tom, of the new baby coming and her present fought-for happiness.

In small groups, discuss this last sentence/paragraph of the novel. Make a list of the words that make it such a good closing to a story.

Endings of other language texts apart from stories are equally important. With a partner write down where these endings come from:

– … we'll be back at ten o'clock, but for now, it's goodnight from me. Goodnight.

– … I repeat, we must catch this pair before they strike again, so, if you have any information phone me or my colleagues on 0148 769769. That's 0148 769769. Thank you.

– … a long ball through the middle beat the offside trap and Jones made it two. United's heads dropped, and there was no way back. This result might mean the drop for them, but for City it all looks rosy.

– …Yeah …All right … No, that's fine … I'll be there … No problem …You just wait … Are you still there? Sorry, it went all fuzzy for a moment – signal must be weak. Anyway, I'll be there at 10 – at Terminal 1, by the flight desk for Kanga Airlines. All right. Bye.

– Kept to my bed today. Doctor came – usual glum predictions – said I shouldn't book any holidays. As if I would, at my age and condition! Still, too tired to write now. I can hear the church bell in the village. Reminds me of my childhood – singing in the choir. Good times. Anyway, should stop now. That doctor's a real tyrant – better do as I'm told.

– Well, Miss Macdonald, I think that's all. Thank you for coming all this way. We've got all your details so we should be in touch by the end of next week. We still have several other people to see, but I can tell you that we are very interested in you. My assistant will show you out. Goodbye – and have a safe journey home.

– Game Over. New Game? Quit?

Now, write down how you know. What special features of language give it away?

 Alice has promised to let her friend, Susan, borrow her ice-skates for a competition. At the last moment, she deliberately lets her down, and Susan has to drop out of the competition. Susan plans her revenge. Write the closing to this story.

Further work and revision

 Go to the library and look at the closings of at least six novels. Choose which you think is the best one. Prepare a short talk to the class about why you feel the closing you have chosen is so good.

 Underline all the adjectives in the *Hush-a-bye* passage and write them down.

Narrative links

> *A chain of events is a story. 'The King died, and then the Queen died', is a story, but not an interesting one. This is because it has only a beginning and an ending. It does not have a middle.*

Beginning

The King died

Ending

and then the Queen died.

To be interesting, a story has to have a middle. We can predict – think what might happen, and why. The middle might explain why and how the King died, why and how the Queen died, and if these two events are linked.

The possible causes of the King's death might be interesting. But the possible causes of the Queen's death are even more intriguing:

The Queen died. Was it murder?
Because somebody else wanted to take over the throne perhaps ...

Was it suicide?
Because of her grief and loneliness ... or had she been somehow involved in the King's death and her guilt tormented her ...

Or?

Read these possible middles carefully.

Beginning	Middle	End
The King died ...	and three weeks later, the Queen married a handsome young prince. Exactly a year after remarrying, while out hunting with the prince and his younger brother ...	the Queen died.
The King died ...	and the Queen lived alone in a remote tower of the castle, almost entirely refusing to eat ...	the Queen died.
The King died ...	but the Queen refused to admit defeat in the war which had raged for the past fifteen years. The war continued to drag on, draining the country of men and prosperity. Finally exhausted ...	the Queen died.

In groups, discuss what might have happened to the King and Queen in each of these three situations. Ask yourselves:

– Why did the Queen choose to remarry a handsome young prince?
– Why did she choose to live alone in a remote tower of the castle?
– Why did she choose to let the war continue?

Write up notes on each situation. Give your reasons in no more than 150 words.

 On your own, decide on the story. Draw a storyboard of at least ten pictures. Cut out the pictures and rearrange them. Get a friend to tell a story based on your selection. Then tell your version using your original selection.

Further work and revision

 Choose one of the above situations and write it up as a complete story. Make sure you have a good beginning, middle and end.

 Using a thesaurus, look up synonyms for the words 'King' and 'Queen'. Write a brief explanation of how the words from the thesaurus differ in meaning.

Summarising

> *A summary is a brief account of the main ideas in a piece of writing. "Tell me, briefly, what it's all about," – that's a summary.*

To summarise:

Understand
- reread the passage
- underline or list key words and ideas
- make rough notes.

Write
- write one or two sentences that get across the basic ideas
- write a rough draft (check that it covers the main ideas and words)
- write your final version.

<u>Katie Summers</u>, a 12-year-old Hampton Park <u>school pupil</u>, has compiled <u>poems</u> about cats, dogs, guinea pigs, horses, cows and <u>many</u> other <u>creatures</u>. "I have been <u>selling</u> the pamphlets to family and friends for 75p each and all the money raised will be donated to a donkey sanctuary," she said. She wants to sell enough copies of her poems to raise money for other animal charities as well, and hopes that her writing talent will help her do this. "I love animals and I love writing poems. I would like to be an author or poet – that is what I hope to be."

Tasks

 How many times have you reread the passage?

 Copy out the passage and underline or list the key words and ideas. We have underlined some for you.

 Copy and complete these rough notes. For example:
Katie wants to be a poet.
Loves ...   animals.
Wants ...   to raise money for animals.

 Now copy and complete this rough draft:

A young pupil, who loves poetry and animals, is selling books of her poems about animals to raise money for ...

 Check it for accuracy, then write the final version.

Read this passage about a rare illness:

'Charcot-Marie Tooth disease'

Thirty-four-year-old Dr Trevor Harrison is spearheading a campaign to raise cash for research into a rare muscle wastage condition to which he has personally fallen victim. He was diagnosed as having Charcot-Marie Tooth disease (CMT) a year ago. The condition is usually found in teenage years and rarely at Dr Harrison's time of life, and he now has to use an electric wheelchair to get about. Charcot-Marie Tooth disease (CMT) is slowly progressive and causes deterioration and wastage of the nerves which control muscle function, particularly of the foot and lower leg, as well as hand, finger and forearm muscles. It can cause chronic pain and extreme tiredness. But Dr Harrison has not been deterred from carrying on his work. He said: "Very little is known about the disease or even about its causes and even less about a cure which is why the support group for sufferers, CMT International, is holding an awareness week next year." Among the people who have so far donated money to help with research are James and Peter Fudge of Sensory Electrical Devices. Peter Fudge, who has known Dr Harrison professionally for a number of years commented: "Trevor is a long-standing friend of many people in the electrical and electronic sensory field. Now it's time we did something to help him."

 Prepare to write a summary of this passage. Reread the passage several times. Then list key words and ideas. Make your rough notes and write up a rough draft.

Further work and revision

 Write the final version of your summary of the passage.

 The 'Charcot-Marie Tooth Disease' story is written in a single paragraph. Rewrite the passage, putting in paragraphs.

Shaping texts

Speech is sound that makes sense. It is an immediate and effective way of communicating. Writing is marks on the page that make sense. It is a deliberate and effective way to communicate. Each way is appropriate for its task.

Tasks

 Look at the different groupings below. Some of them need rearranging. Re-do the groupings putting the appropriate activities under the correct headings.

Speech and writing

Holiday postcard

Asking someone the time

Giving instructions to your captain during a sports match

Giving directions

Leaving a will

Sports report

Telling the time

Warning someone about to cross a road

Writing

Ordering a pizza

Applying for a job

Enquiring about a job

Leaving a message before you go out

Shopping list

Asking your mum for more pocket money

Telling another player to pass the ball to you in a game

Wedding speech

Speech

Job contract

Job interview

Plans to build a house

Telling a child off

Asking for a bus ticket

Crossword

10 000-name petition

School exams

Read this dialogue (in pairs) between Mr and Mrs Cowdrey at breakfast:

Mr Cowdrey:	Dear Mrs Cowdrey, I am speaking from the end of the breakfast table from where it is somewhat difficult to reach the toast. I would be grateful if you could pass it to me.
Mrs Cowdrey:	Thank you for your kind request, Mr Cowdrey. I will make every effort to deal with the problem as soon as I have removed a slice myself.
Mr Cowdrey:	With all due respect, I will be late for work.
Mrs Cowdrey:	If that is the case, I suggest you deal with the matter yourself and use those limbs attached to the bottom half of your body.

Discuss what is inappropriate about this conversation:

How is it different from normal speech?

Copy it out and rewrite the verbs with 'I' or 'you' as a contraction, for example 'I am' = 'I'm'.

Does it sound better?

Make any other improvements and then do a final version in best.

 Continue Mr and Mrs Cowdrey's conversation using polite and rather 'artificial' language.

Further work and revision

 Your neighbours, Mr and Mrs Cowdrey, are upset because you have played music too loudly when your parents were out.

In pairs:
- Role-play a telephone conversation in which you apologise to Mr or Mrs Cowdrey.
- Write a letter of apology to them.
- Discuss which means of communication you found most effective and why. Write a paragraph giving your reasons.

 List the most important points of your letter of apology.

Accent and dialect

Accent is how we say something. Here are some well-known accents:

West Midlands ('Brummie')

Australian

Received Pronunciation, sometimes called 'BBC' English

Welsh

London ('Cockney')

Newcastle ('Geordie')

Jamaican

Tasks

1   Write down any more accents you can think of.

Here is a poem written to show accent. It was written by Barry Heath, who lives in the county of Nottinghamshire.

First Day at School

it wurorribul m'fost
day a schooil
memate jeff flewit
went wime
an teacha wunt lerrus
sit next tureachother

went shiwent aht
cockut class cumup
t'me
ansed, "AH canfaityo
cahnt ah?"
an ah sed eecudunt
an ee sed ee cud
an ah sed ee cuddent
an eeit me
so ah itim back just
as teacha cumin

shipicked up that
stick as y'point
at bord'we
an crackt m'ovver
edweeit
an sed, "Widontav
ooligunsere."

so ah went omm at
playtime an towd
memam
an memam took meback
t'school agen
owdin metab

Barry Heath

In groups, read the poem out loud. Who in the group can say the poem most accurately? Discuss the effects of using an accent in this way in a poem.

A dialect is a local version of language which may use its own words. Barry Heath's poem *First Day at School* uses only one dialect word 'tab' (which means 'ear'). Here is an extract from a poem by Robert Burns, written in Scottish dialect, which uses many more dialect words:

> My curse upon your venom'd stang
> That shoots my tortured gums alang;
> And thr' my lugs gies monie a twang,
> Wi' gnawing vengeance;
> Tearing my nerves wi' bitter pang,
> Like racking engines!

Write down what you think this poem is about, then write it out in your own words. Make a list of the words that you find difficult.

 Read *Restroom Rap* now, and then copy out the dialect words in italics and write down what they mean in your own words. What dialect is being used here?

Restroom Rap

I was crunching my *chips* the other day
I was sitting on the *hood* of my Chevrolet
I polished my *fender* till it shone like new,
The mirror, the door, my large *trunk* too.

Out of the *restroom* a cool *chick* came,
She said, "Hey *buddy*, what's your name?
The *faucet*'s broken, I need a hand,
Can you change a *diaper*? My baby's damp.'

Took off my *tuxedo*, in I went,
Said, 'Hey pretty mama, I'm heaven sent!'
But that there job was too tough for me,
I'll stick to *homicide* and robbery!

Bongo Lee and *Eartha Closit*

Further work and revision

 Write out *First Day at School* in standard English, using standard spelling, punctuation and capitals. Which version do you prefer – Barry Heath's or the corrected one? Write two short paragraphs explaining your reasons.

 Summarise what *First Day at School* is about.

Shaping texts

Children's language/adults' language

Language develops as we grow older and we learn to use it in different ways. Children's language often expresses strong emotions. Adults' language more often deals with communicating information and ideas.

Read this poem:

Writing
and then i saw it
saw it all   all the mess
and blood and evrythink
and mam agenst the kitchin dor
the flor all stiky
and the wall all wet
and red an dad besid the kichen draw
i saw it saw it all
an wrot it down an ever word of it is tru

You must take care to write in sentences.
Check your spellings and your paragraphs.
Is this finished? It is rather short.
Perhaps next time you will have more to say.

Jan Dean

Tasks

1 In pairs, discuss what has happened in this poem. Make a list of the key incidents. Write down how you would feel if the teacher had written these comments (the ones in italics) on your work.

2 Imagine you are a police officer called to deal with the incident that the pupil describes. Write a brief factual report on what has happened.

3 Read this poem:

Mummy Tells Joseph about the Princess

Mummy told him the flag draped across the coffin –
A blanket to keep her cold body warm in.
He nodded, he understood:
This was life, this was good.

Mummy told him the flowers strewn across the ways ahead –
A token to keep her fragrant in her fast bed.
He nodded, he understood:
This was life, this was good.

Mummy told him the magic Princess was really dead –
He sensed the shock, felt how loss, grief spread.
He nodded, he understood:
This was life, this was good.

Mummy told him, best she could, what death means –
His favourite film was Sleeping Beauty's magic scene.
He nodded, he understood:
This was life, this was good.

"Mummy", he cried, trying to help her explain –
"The Prince will kiss her lips – then, then she'll wake again".
He nodded, he understood:
This was life, this was good.

James Sale

In small groups discuss the following:

– What does the young child think when he sees the coffin?
– How does the child think he is helping his mother?
– What situations did you find difficult to make sense of as a young child?
– Was it easier to talk to other children or to adults when you were young?
– In what ways has your language developed over the years?

Further work and revision

4 Write your diary entry for either the best or the worst day in your life. Use the diary entry to write a short article called *The Best/Worst Day of My Life* for your school magazine. The style will probably need to change between the two.

5 Rewrite Jan Dean's poem as prose, using capitals, paragraphs and correct spellings. Write a brief paragraph saying which works better – the corrected version, or the original. Explain your reasons.

Tests and longer assignments

The following two pages focus mainly on longer assignments based on skills covered in Section 4. Part One contains one short test and two other compulsory tasks; Part Two gives a choice of two assignments.

Part One: Compulsory

 Copy out and rewrite the following sentences so that they make sense:

- definitely will later it rain
- coming the last to the town circus was at
- alloys bike used new titanium his incredibly the and light was
- only spell-check the to on this is if how spell computer you great know but
- grammar practical this to some guide is important most book elements a of the of

 The following article should be written in three short paragraphs. Decide where the paragraphs should be and copy out the article, adding full-stops, capitals, speech marks and paragraph indentations where necessary. Give the article a short title of no more than six words.

in letters to newspapers and in messages on the internet, ordinary people wrote about princess diana as a light shining in people's hearts; more like the girl next door than a member of the royal family; a friend even though I had never met her the singer george michael described her as truly the greatest ambassador for compassion and humanity in modern times others had special memories philip woolcock, whose 19-year-old daughter had been comforted by diana princess of wales just a week before she died of cancer, and who had subsequently met her, said: she spoke to us with an honesty and compassion that we hitherto had not experienced from anybody vincent seabrook, a 27-year-old security man whom princess diana had befriended when he was homeless, said she had saved his life: you have a very caring heart, and I will never forget you, he wrote on a hand-made plaque he left at kensington palace sarah, widow of hugh lindsay, the prince of wales's friend killed in an avalanche on a holiday with the prince and princess, recalled what she called diana's remarkable kindness she had this incredible ability to make you feel you were important, she said

3 Copy out the following article so that the paragraphs are in the correct order:

– She went on to add that the Government was considering bringing in tough new laws so that councils could get rid of residents who make too much noise.

– Noise has been a particular problem in Eastville. In the last month alone there have been over a hundred complaints about people playing music too loud, arguing, shouting and generally ruining their neighbours' quality of life.

– The Government declared war on noisy neighbours today. In a speech, MP Rhona MacFadden said that it was time that people could live their lives in peace.

– "We've had enough," said a resident who didn't want to be named. "They should be told to move – and their houses given to law-abiding people."

Part Two

Choose one of the following:

 1 Read the following extract. Imagine you are a seven-year-old child who has witnessed the events. Write your account of what happened.

I am police constable 8392, based at Grundy Hill station, Foreham. At about a quarter to ten on the morning of the sixth of April I was travelling in my vehicle and in the direction of Troop on the A361 in the county of Wiltshire. I noticed some way ahead of me that the traffic had been brought to a halt by what appeared to have been a road traffic accident. When I arrived at the scene I immediately saw that two men were engaged in a dispute and that their behaviour to each other appeared to be violent. It was then that I contacted my station headquarters by radio, requesting support from any other police officers in the area. Two vehicles, which it later transpired belonged to the two men I saw at the scene, had both been quite severely damaged in the accident and were across the grass verge next to the road at that place. I tried to calm the two men and to separate them, at which point one of the men, the defendant, Mr Jones, said to me: "Just go away, copper, you ain't got nothing to do with this." I informed Mr Jones that he was in breach of the peace and liable to be arrested for his unruly behaviour. The other man, Mr Smith, then said to Mr Jones: "I'll do you for this, you git," and attempted to strike Mr Jones with a blow to the face. Mr Jones retaliated with a head-butt in the direction of Mr Smith, which, however, caught me a striking blow to the side of the face, causing my cap to fall to the ground. I again tried to separate the two men and in the ensuing violence I suffered a broken nose and severely cut lip, for which I required hospital treatment.

 2 Write a short story, using these sentences as the first and last. Give your story a title.

Opening sentence: **It was a bleak cold day in November and dry autumn leaves were being blown high in the dull sky by the bitter wind …**

Closing sentence: **I turned and closed the door behind me. I knew I'd never return.**

Setting personal targets

 Look through the work you did in Section 4 and make a list of the things you did not understand or did not do very well. Keep your list to refer to.

 Talk to your teacher and choose at least three and no more than five of the following targets to meet. Make sure you choose reading, writing and speaking and listening targets. Use your list to help you choose.

Titles

● I will look at the titles of past stories I have written and check to see if my titles were the best possible ones.

Paragraphs

● I will check my work to make sure I have used paragraphs in it.
● I will check my paragraphs by counting how many sentences each paragraph contains. I will try to vary the number of sentences in a paragraph from 1–6 sentences, where appropriate.

Verses

● I have studied verses containing four lines. I will go to the library and take out and read a good poetry anthology. I will identify poems with verses of two, three and five lines. I will write down the names of the poems in my exercise book or folder.
● I will try to write poems with different verse patterns: I will try to write at least one poem with verses of three or five lines.

Openings and Closings

● I will spend time in the library reading the opening and closing sentences/paragraphs of various novels/short stories. I will collect examples of the best ones I find and copy them into my exercise book or folder.
● When I next write a story I shall pay particular attention to the opening/closing sentences.

Differences between written and spoken English

● I will pay attention when I speak – I shall try to be clear and precise, especially in formal situations. I will ask other people – friends/teachers/parents/others – for some feedback on how I talk.

Summarising

- I will keep a list of all the titles of fiction books I read. Alongside each one I will write a short summary of what each book is about.
- I will read the local newspaper this week, find a report on a topic I care about, and summarise it.

Predicting

- When I have read the first two or three chapters of a novel, I will write a brief prediction of what I think will happen in the rest of the story.

Accent and dialect

- I will search in the library for poems written in dialect. I will perform the best one to a friend/my class/a parent.

Children's language/adults' language

- I will listen carefully to children and adults speaking, and especially to anybody from another part of this country. I will try to notice the vocabulary they use, and how their language helps them with their expression.
- I have a young brother/sister/next-door neighbour/friend's young brother/sister and I will jot down things they say which seem different or surprising. I will keep a log for a week.

Index